The
Ocean Hero
Handbook

The Ocean Hero Handbook

Simple things you can do to save our seas

TESSA WARDLEY
Illustrated by **Mélanie Johnsson**

IVY PRESS

First published in the UK and North America in 2022 by
Ivy Press
An imprint of The Quarto Group
The Old Brewery, 6 Blundell Street
London N7 9BH, United Kingdom
T (0)20 7700 6700
www.Quarto.com

British Library Cataloguing-in-Publication Data
A catalogue record for this book is available from the British Library.

ISBN: 978-0-7112-6625-4

Printed in China

10 9 8 7 6 5 4 3 2 1

Contents

Foreword   6

Introduction   9

1. Indoors   **12**

2. Outdoors   **32**

3. Transport   **54**

4. On Holiday   **70**

5. At Work   **84**

6. Food & Shopping   **96**

7. Clothes   **116**

Conclusion   134

References   136

Index   142

Acknowledgements   144

Foreword

The ocean is our greatest natural asset: we rely on it for food and water, to support biodiversity, and for climate stability – we cannot tackle climate change without a healthy ocean. Yet inexplicably we take it for granted, abuse its resources and seem to be doing our best to destroy it. Something has to change, and change starts with individual responsibility. *The Ocean Hero Handbook* empowers every one of us to play our part in taking action towards saving our ocean, and helps to show us how.

As an endurance swimmer, I have had the great privilege of immersing myself in the wonder and beauty that is our ocean. I have experienced the magnificent creatures that live there and the majesty of our blue planet. I have also been exposed to the greatest tragedies: swimming around bleached corals, through discarded plastic, over the watery deserts created by overfishing, dredging and pollution, and across waters that until recently were solid glaciers. I have witnessed the devastating impact that we humans are having, putting our ocean and every organism on earth that relies on it in danger. The disastrous impact of our actions – out of sight and out of mind for many – is evident throughout the ocean; no part of this last great wilderness is safe.

The love I have for the ocean, and the tragedies I have witnessed, have made me the advocate I am today. I have made it my mission to highlight the impact we are having on our ocean, and to encourage governments and administrations to turn the tide on plastic pollution, to protect our seas from overexploitation, disturbance, and climate change.

The good news is that marine species and habitats have demonstrated their ability to bounce back and recover when we give them a bit of space. And to help them find that space I am working with the United Nations and my Lewis Pugh Foundation to champion marine protected areas (MPAs), which restrict commercial fishing activities and provide protection from other pressures, in order to set up the conditions in which marine ecosystems can recover.

Well-managed MPAs result in healthy and diverse ecosystems, which provide a wide range of benefits for people and the planet, locally and globally. These include:

• Resilience against factors such as disease, global warming, pollution, and the increasingly extreme weather events that we can't always anticipate and prevent.
• A natural wilderness we can all enjoy, providing economic value through tourism, and academic value through developing our understanding of how natural systems work and future medical and technological resources that we cannot yet predict.
• Food security. As fish and larvae thrive in the MPAs, they support marine ecosystems and fish populations beyond, maintaining local fish supplies for the millions of people globally who rely on this important source of food.

I speak to governments and institutions around the world, working to influence decision-makers to protect our ocean, but I know that will not be enough. People hold the power to drive change: passionate people, ordinary people, stepping up and making a million small changes in their own lives, every day, all of which add up to make a big difference. It is consumer power that will influence the actions of businesses and persuade governments to legislate for the new normal. And it is up to every one of us to play our part in making these changes happen.

As I said in my World Oceans Day message in 2021, 'Every day we make decisions about what we eat, how we travel to school or work, the clothes we wear or how we warm our homes. And ultimately, all these choices impact our oceans.' I went on to urge everyone to ask themselves a simple question: what changes can you make today to help save our ocean?

This little book helps to answer that big question. Alongside the shocking statistics and headlines that highlight the devastating impacts that can be seen in our marine environments right now, are suggestions about the changes you can make today, and how you too can be an ocean hero.

I urge you to read this book, make the right choices, talk to your friends about what you are doing, and encourage them to join us. Collectively, we can help deliver the transformational change needed to save our ocean and all the life on earth that depends on it.

Lewis Pugh, OIG
UN Patron of the Oceans

Introduction

Those who had the privilege of seeing our planet from space for the first time named it the 'Blue Marble'. Seen from a distance, the importance of our ocean is abundantly clear: covering 71 per cent of the earth in a big blue blanket, it contains around 97 per cent of our planet's water; 40 per cent of our global population live within 100 kilometres of a land/ocean boundary; it provides more than 90 per cent of the living space for all of our planet's species; and delivers 50 per cent of the oxygen we breathe.

And there is so much more to explore and understand. More people have walked on the moon and seen the ocean from space than have visited its deepest parts. The ocean is our least explored wilderness, whose mystery and adventure draws many to the water's edge.

Many of us feel an emotional attachment to our blue spaces; there is much evidence to demonstrate that being by, on or in the water enhances our mood, helping to combat anxiety and depression. Even just thinking about watery environments can have an impact on how we feel – soothing our minds and enhancing our wellbeing. But the ocean is considerably more fundamental to our survival than the role it plays in providing a setting for our leisure activities and contributing to our welfare – it is an integral component of our climate control system. Through the global exchange of water, energy, and carbon, it keeps our world in dynamic equilibrium, balancing our water supplies, weather patterns, and the air we breathe.

Without a healthy ocean there can be no life on earth. Yet despite the global climate and biodiversity emergency finally reaching the top of the political agenda, it seems that the ocean is not part of the narrative – it is poorly articulated or understood beyond the scientific community.

Ocean warming, caused by climate change, can initiate climate feedback systems, leading it to reach irreversible thresholds of change. Around 10 per cent of the global population live at less than 10 metres above sea level and are at risk from rising sea levels. However, 100 per cent of the global population are at risk from the extreme weather events caused by the impacts of climate change on the ocean.

By protecting our ocean, we will bolster our planet's climate resilience. Mangroves, kelp forests, and seagrass meadows along the margins, and plankton in the millions of square kilometres of open ocean, all absorb carbon from the atmosphere. Controlling ocean warming will minimize extreme weather events and encourage biodiversity.

Protecting our ocean's biodiversity from plastics, pollution, overfishing and mining impacts enhances food and job security. Billions of us globally rely on fish for protein and livelihoods; the economic benefits of protecting just 30 per cent of our ocean is estimated to run into hundreds of billions of dollars.[1] We owe it to ourselves and our future on this planet to help our ocean, and we will be repaid many times over by the ecosystem support services delivered through food and water supply, clean air, renewable energy, and benefits for health and wellbeing, cultural values, tourism, trade, and transport.

We know that business as usual is not an option: governments, policy-makers, lobbyists, business leaders, and every one of us in our everyday lives must be a part of the transformative change required to bring us back from the brink of catastrophic climate change and biodiversity loss. Our ocean crosses national boundaries and we need coordinated global action and international agreements to protect it. So, what is our role?

We can speak truth to power and support action with climate strikes, choosing leaders who believe in international action on the environment. But there is more we can do through our everyday choices and behaviour. As new generations grow up on our planet, nature depleted and climate unstable, we can make certain choices.

David Attenborough inspired a generation to look beyond the impact we are having on the land and to think about what we release into our blue planet. We now take reusable water bottles to school and work and we shun plastic bags in the supermarket, but there is so much more we can do. This book will help to highlight the actions and choices that are impacting our oceans, seas, and coastal waters, and to champion some amazing and hopeful initiatives that aim to deliver a change to the narrative. Rather than something we can plunder and exploit, we should see the ocean as part of us and our everyday activities, as important to our survival as the air we breathe – every second breath of which comes courtesy of the ocean.

We need to 'think ocean' as we go about our day, and make our choices with the ocean in mind. It is time we all played the role of ocean hero.

Chapter 1

Indoors

Around 42,000 tons of plastic from personal care products finds its way into the ocean every year

THE ISSUE

At least 8 million tons of plastic ends up in the ocean every year, making up 80 per cent of all marine rubbish.[2] Plastics in the ocean cause a problem for wildlife and humans: marine species ingest or are entangled in plastic debris, and plastic pollution threatens our food safety and health.

WHAT CAN WE DO?

Less than 10 per cent of the plastic produced globally is currently recycled, and it has been estimated that only 50 per cent of bathroom plastics are recycled compared with 90 per cent in the kitchen.[3]

Take a look in your bathroom cabinet and think about which beauty products you actually need, and which are just cluttering up your shelves. Of those that are left, is there an alternative to the plastic container? Bars of soap, shampoo, and conditioner wrapped in paper can easily replace plastic bottles of liquid soap and hair products. And if you really can't get along with bars, then try to find refillable options so you don't need a new bottle every month. Look for alternatives to plastic toothpaste tubes – the vast majority are made from mixed plastics and can't be recycled. Try powders that come in tins, or toothpaste and mouthwash tablets that come in refillable jars.

Sanitary towels and tampons contain plastics, particularly if they have plastic applicators – think about a menstrual cup, which reduces virtually all plastic waste.

WHY IT MATTERS

300 million tons of plastic are produced annually[4], creating a huge carbon footprint and leading to ocean warming and sea level rise as a consequence of climate change.

Baby-care products are stealing your baby's – and the ocean's – future

THE ISSUE

An estimated 3 billion nappies are thrown away in the UK each year – your baby alone can poop its way through around 4–6000![5] Disposable nappies and wipes can take up to 500 years to decompose, leaching plastics and chemicals into the environment all the time.[6]

WHAT CAN WE DO?

By choosing reusable nappies, we retain control over our carbon and pollution emissions. Most of the environmental impacts associated with disposables are in their manufacture (beyond our control), whereas the impacts from reusables are dependent on our own behaviour – washing, drying, and length of use. You will only need 20–30 reusables in your whole baby's nappy-using life and you can use them for the next baby too.

If a complete move to reusables is a step too far, try using them daytime only or when you are at home. And for those single-use nappies you don't manage to cut out, there are biodegradable options on the market. They will still take the rest of your lifetime to biodegrade, but they are a massive improvement on disposables.

In 2017, wipes came in at number seven in the top ten waste products found on beaches. They are also a major component of fatbergs that clog up our sewers, causing overflow directly into the environment. Reusable cloths do the job, can go in the wash with the nappies, and are much better than reaching for disposable wipes.[7]

WHY IT MATTERS

In 2008, the UK Environment Agency observed that the behaviour around how we wash and dry reusables, and whether they are in fact reused for subsequent children, can reduce our carbon footprint by up to 40 per cent.[8]

There are 500 times more microplastics in our ocean than stars in our galaxy

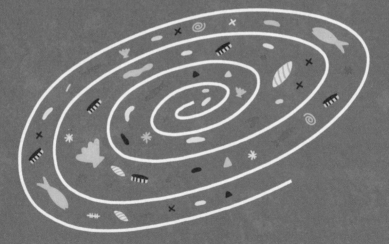

THE ISSUE

Microplastics are particles of plastic, less than 5mm in size. Scientists have discovered microplastics contaminating marine environments all over the world, including deep in the Arctic ice and ocean trenches. They are also found in one in three fish caught for human consumption.[9]

WHAT CAN WE DO?

Some personal care products, such as shower gels, moisturizers, and deodorants, intentionally contain microbeads. Microbead concentrations in products such as exfoliants can be so great that the product contains more plastic than the packaging.[10] Increasingly, these microbeads are being banned (e.g. in the UK, Canada, and Europe), but keep your eye on the ingredients of your beauty products to make sure they are not there.

Be vigilant with products that used to contain microbeads – check they are not just substituting smaller nano plastics that could be equally damaging and even harder to remove in sewage treatment. Ingredients to avoid include (but are not limited to): polypropylene, polyethylene, polystyrene, polyurethane, polyacrylate, butylene, and nylon.

Other sources of microplastics in the ocean are entirely unintentional, coming from the synthetic polymers in car tyres (see page 62) and the plastic fibres in our clothes (see page 120).

WHY IT MATTERS

It is estimated that 1.5–3.2 million tons, 15–31, per cent of all ocean plastics come from microplastics. Our global releases of microplastics are equivalent to every single person throwing an empty shopping bag into the sea every week of the year.[11]

Domestic energy consumption plays a role in rising sea levels

THE ISSUE

Carbon emissions associated with energy use contribute to climate change, which results in ocean warming, melting ice sheets, and rising sea levels. And with 10 per cent of the global population living at less than 10 metres above sea level, people's homes and lives are at risk.

....

WHAT CAN WE DO?

Replacing old incandescent light bulbs as they wear out with light emitting diode (LED) and compact fluorescent light (CFL) bulbs uses less energy, and will save you money in the long run as they last longer and use less electricity. Make sure unused tech is unplugged. And when you replace white goods, check out the energy rating stickers to keep your electricity consumption to the minimum.

Turn your heating down a notch in winter and put on a cosy jumper, and in summer don't rely so much on the aircon. Make your house super-efficient by installing double glazing and insulating cavity walls and loft spaces. Again, this will save money in the long run but it can have an up-front cost – check out government grants and allowances.

Change your electricity supplier to a renewable-only supplier. Electricity from renewable sources (wind, sun, water, and wood) outperformed production from gas and coal plants in Europe and the UK throughout the whole of 2020 for the first time and is set to do the same in 2021.[12]

WHY IT MATTERS

In the European Union, buildings consume 40 per cent of all energy produced and emit 36 per cent of total CO_2 emissions.[13] In the United States, residential energy use accounts for roughly 20 per cent of greenhouse gas emissions.[14]

Online data storage is heating the seas

THE ISSUE

Carbon is emitted to deliver our every stream, scroll, and tap, and data centres produce so much heat that they need to be cooled. Some have even been submerged in coastal areas to use the ocean's cooling powers.[15]

. . . .

WHAT CAN WE DO?

The internet is a great way to communicate, but we need to reduce our impact. A single email may produce 4 grams of carbon emissions, but this can reach 50 grams if it includes a large attachment[16], so link to documents instead, and only send emails to those who really need to see them.

A one-minute phone call is only a little more consumptive than sending a text – the least carbon-hungry way to message – but a video call has a much higher carbon footprint. This should be balanced against the effect of travelling to get together, however: a car journey exceeds the carbon emissions of a video call after less than 20 kilometres, so if you're any further than that, make it a video call.[17]

Cut emissions by downloading rather than streaming content, watching on wi-Fi rather than 4G, and watching with family and friends rather than on separate devices. And make sure you close tabs so they don't continue playing when you stop watching and listening.

Gaming also has environmental costs. One study found that US gamers used 2.4 per cent of their annual household electricity – more than the freezer or washing machine.[18]

WHY IT MATTERS

The energy we use on our online activities each year is around 4 per cent of all global emissions – and this is set to double by 2025.[19]

Chemicals from cleaning products have been found in dolphins

THE ISSUE
Every time we rinse off the chemicals we use to keep our homes and bodies clean, we risk them getting into our rivers and soils and ultimately washing into our seas and ocean.

....

WHAT CAN WE DO?
Switching cleaning products can have a big impact on our ocean. Have a look at your bottles to learn more about what is in there. As well as the usual hazard warnings about the harms they could do to us, many display the additional alarming message: 'harmful to aquatic life with long-lasting effects'. While these refer to concentrated releases direct to the environment, there are plenty of alternatives we can choose that don't have these associated risks. Try to avoid:

• Anything that is marked 'danger' or 'poison', 'caution' or 'warning'.

• Products that don't list the ingredients; if ingredients are recorded, avoid phthalates, phosphates, phenols, methylisothiazolinone, and triclosan.

• Overuse of antibacterial products. As well as having a toxic effect on marine life, their use is contributing to antibiotic resistance'.

Good cleaning products contain ingredients that are non-toxic to wildlife – they may be labelled as 'biodegradable' or 'environment-friendly'.

WHY IT MATTERS
Phthalates are endocrine disruptors, affecting reproduction and neurology in aquatic life.[20] Studies have found high levels in over 70 per cent of dolphins studied in Florida.[21]

Household DIY and car maintenance are killing coastal seagrass and kelp beds

THE ISSUE

The drains in our gardens and on the kerbside don't go through sewage treatment and typically discharge straight to watercourses. DIY and car clean-up often happens outside, adding to the pollutant load.

WHAT CAN WE DO?

Don't tip excess paint and white spirit down the drain! You will need to harden water-soluble paint before disposal as waste centres are unable to accept liquid paint, while white spirit and solvent-based paints and thinners should be disposed of as hazardous substances. Check to see what your local recycling centre accepts.

When we wash our cars, dirty water containing detergents, exhaust residue, gasoline, heavy metals from rust, and motor oils eventually end up in the ocean. Try to wash your car on a surface that absorbs water, such as gravel or grass, to filter it before it enters the drain. Use biodegradable, phosphate-free, water-based cleaners and empty buckets into sinks or toilets so they are going into the treatment system.

If you are changing motor oil, never tip it down a drain. Collect it in a leakproof container with a secure lid and take it to your nearest recycling centre. If you have a spill, stop it from entering the drain by mixing it with sand or soil – bag up the material and dispose of it as contaminated waste.

WHY IT MATTERS

Seagrasses account for 10–18 per cent of the ocean's annual carbon storage[22]; they release oxygen and capture carbon up to 35 times faster than rainforests. In the UK alone, around 92 per cent of seagrass meadows have been destroyed in the last century.

Why are plastics such a problem for our ocean?

Plastic is a miracle material: cheap, flexible, transparent, and inert, it has transformed our world, from facilitating medical treatments to reducing food waste. But there is a downside: this fossil-fuelled, indestructible product is killing our ocean.

Over 300 million tons of plastic are produced every year from petroleum, using around 8 per cent of our global supplies – and half of that plastic is used once and then thrown away.

We have all seen pictures of vast islands of plastic accumulating in the middle of the ocean, caught in circulating currents or gyres. One, known as the Great Pacific Garbage Patch, is thought to be twice the size of France and still growing. Plastics make up the majority of all marine litter – at least 8 million tons of plastic end up in our ocean every year (some estimates put it as high as 15 million tons) – and it has been found on the shorelines of every continent. Most of it is washed out of our drains, dropped by beach visitors, or escaped from poorly managed waste.

The trouble with this indestructible material is that it stays around for hundreds of years, and when solar UV radiation, wind, and water do take their toll, it just breaks up into smaller and smaller pieces; it never disappears.

Why is it important?

Alarming images of sea life entangled in plastic, and dead animals with stomachs full of plastic bags, clearly illustrate the dangers of discarded plastic. They are the shocking outcomes of marine birds, mammals, fish, and turtles mistaking marine debris for food, causing them to starve or suffocate. They also cause cuts and injuries and provide a substrate via which disease organisms can spread, as well as transport invasive species between land masses and around the ocean.

Not all plastic in the ocean is visible – an estimated 94 per cent lies deep below the surface, disturbing ocean habitats and disrupting ecosystems. A further proportion, known as microplastics, are so small that they can be invisible to the naked eye. Some are washed into the ocean as clothing fibres and tyre dust, or originate from single-use plastics, which break down into smaller particles as they degrade. Tiny particles of plastic are now so common that they have been identified in samples of seawater, plants, and animals in every corner of the ocean.

Plastic in seawater absorbs chemicals, and there are chemicals used in plastic production, all of which are known to be carcinogenic and interfere with the body's endocrine systems.[23] These chemicals, ingested by wildlife along with the plastics, accumulate up the food chain and end up in the fish we eat.

Plastic is unsightly and impacts on the appearance and value of tourist destinations. Many coastal regions that rely on tourist income lose money on beach clean-up costs. On top of all that, the use of petroleum as the raw product to make plastics and the large amount of fossil fuel energy use in production has a massive carbon footprint, contributing directly to ocean warming and reducing the ability of the ocean to produce the oxygen we rely on to breathe.

Inspirational actions on plastics

Spending time in, on or around the ocean inspires people. The vast wonder and beauty of the water and the wildlife it supports raises awe in those who spend time immersed in its power. The damage we are doing to this wilderness is also brought into sharp focus, and the need to take action to protect it becomes urgent and all-encompassing – to limit and reverse the impact of man.

Three people who have been so inspired by their close encounters with the ocean that they have devoted their lives to changing the way we treat it are Dame Ellen MacArthur, Lewis Pugh, and Tom Kay. We can draw strength and encouragement from the voices these activists and supporters present, as well as using what they have learnt to help drive the transformational change in the way we treat our ocean.

Solo long-distance yachtswoman and former world record holder for the fastest solo circumnavigation of the globe, Dame Ellen MacArthur has witnessed the majesty and the might of the ocean up close and bore witness to the finite nature of our planet's resources. Inspired to act, she has set up the Ellen MacArthur Foundation to develop and promote the idea of a circular economy, working with business, academia, policy-makers, and institutions to design waste and pollution out of our systems and keep products and materials in use.

Lewis Pugh, pioneering swimmer, ocean advocate, and UN Patron of the Ocean, has experienced extreme adventures in the coldest corners of our ocean. Inspired by the beauty and shocked by the impacts of climate change, overfishing, and plastic pollution, he now swims to raise awareness for the ocean.

His message is clear: we are in a race against time to save our ocean, and full and proper marine-protected areas offer our best hope for recovery. He has founded the Lewis Pugh Foundation to help unite governments, NGOs, scientific institutions and world citizens around a common cause: to preserve our ocean for a peaceful and sustainable future.

B Corp clothing company Finisterre was born from the needs of Atlantic surfers. Tom Kay developed the company ethos through a love of the sea passed down from his parents. The company focuses on functional solutions that 'warm cold souls fresh from the sea'. Its clothing pushes boundaries, pioneering new technologies and novel ocean-side clothing solutions – recycling fishing nets and ocean plastics and championing an ocean-friendly way of life. Developing functional and sustainable clothing, the ocean environment runs through its core. An example of the lengths it will go to is in its development (with partners Aquapak) of 'Leave No Trace' garment bags. Water-soluble, recyclable, and biodegradable, these bags are an industry first and break down harmlessly into non-toxic biomass in soil and sea.

B Corp certified businesses meet the most stringent targets for improving the environment and society – when you buy from B Corps you can be sure these businesses have been through a rigorous certification process that has measured their entire social and environmental performance. B Corps help us use business as a force for good; paying much more than lip service, you can be confident they prioritize the environment and society in their operations.

Chapter 2

Outdoors

Fertilizers are creating 'dead zones' in coastal waters around the world

THE ISSUE

About half of all nutrients washed off the land come from fertilizers, fuelling excessive algal growth which create 'dead zones' – oceanic deserts devoid of the usual coastal biodiversity.[24]

....

WHAT CAN WE DO?

Synthetic chemical fertilizers are not the only way to keep soils fertile. Organic alternatives exist that don't put our soil, water, and health at risk.

Under natural conditions, carbon cycling and rotting down of plant mulch keeps our soils productive and healthy, which means fertilizers are not needed. Unfortunately, as we work in our gardens we upset this balance and take more from the soil than we return. Rotating crops in our veg patch and making our own compost will help the structure of the soil and keep it open and aerated, which means available nutrients are accessible to your plants. You can make your own compost from garden clippings and vegetable scraps from the kitchen, which will also save on greenhouse gas emissions from food waste to landfill.

If you can't make your own compost, you can buy organic matter, which may be anything from seaweed, bone meal, municipal composts, poultry or stable manure, and even wastes from paper, brewing, wool, and biodigesters. This is less concentrated than the chemical options, so you need more in volume but they release the nutrients more slowly.

WHY IT MATTERS

More than 60 per cent of coastal rivers and bays in the continental United States are moderately to severely degraded by nutrient pollution.[25]

One calorie of shop-bought food energy takes ten calories of fossil fuel energy to produce[26]

THE ISSUE
From food that is shipped thousands of miles to those wrapped in plastic or treated with chemicals – it all comes at a cost to the ocean.

. . . .

WHAT CAN WE DO?
Use whatever space you have – yard, windowsill, rooftop – to grow your own produce. This reduces your carbon footprint but also gives a sense of agency and reduces feelings of dependency on others. Essentially you are turning energy from the sun into calories through photosynthesis.

A good starting point is salad leaves, which can be sown successionally over a month or two so you have a constant supply, while herbs and microgreens can fit in a small spot on a windowsill.

Once you have got to grips with plants indoors, think about taking it outside – strawberries, currants, and gooseberries are all easy options that can be grown in a pot or plot. Peas are another firm favourite. And think about some of the late summer crops if you have space – squashes and courgettes tend to be prolific and store well.

If you don't have any space at home, there are many community gardening groups or allotment schemes you can join. Think about wildlife too – make sure you don't use any chemicals, and let a small section of the plants flower for the pollinators – they'll liven up your patch as well.

WHY IT MATTERS
The pollution and carbon footprints of our food are damaging the ocean – growing our own reduces our impact, makes us more aware of our own food usage and is great for our mental health.

Destroying natural peatland has a greater impact on ocean climate change and coastal flooding than rainforest destruction

THE ISSUE

Peatland covers 3 per cent of the world's surface and is our largest terrestrial carbon store. It also holds ten times its weight in water, delaying run-off from extreme rainfall events and preventing coastal flooding. Around 15 per cent of the world's peatlands have been drained, for agricultural conversion, burning and mining for fuel, and for compost.[27]

WHAT CAN WE DO?

There is no debate around this one – we must stop using it. Peat is easily replaced by other materials. You can make your own compost or leaf mould or find a larger scale composting operation locally. Bark chippings can also be used, as well as coir and sheep's wool waste. If you go for shop-bought compost, look carefully at the labelling: environmentally friendly and organic do not necessarily mean peat-free.

To replace peat as a soil improver or mulcher, use small quantities of well-rotted animal manure. Your own compost or leaf mould is ideal, as well as wood chips or shavings and bark. You can also create your own green manure by sowing fast-growing plants like rye and alfalfa on bare soil in autumn. The roots help break up heavy soil and suppress weeds, then in spring you can cut them down, leaving the plants on the soil to mulch down, then digging them back into the soil to capture the nutrients.

WHY IT MATTERS

It takes hundreds of years to form just 10 centimetres of peat, as waterlogged vegetation decays slowly – it is therefore not a renewable energy source within the human lifespan.

A decline in insect species threatens our ocean's ecosystem

THE ISSUE
40 per cent of the world's insect species are threatened with extinction. An essential source of food, driving nutrient cycles, pollination, and pest control, their decline threatens our ocean travelling birds and a complete collapse of all natural ecosystems.[28, 29]

....

WHAT CAN WE DO?
By supporting insects in our gardens, we can supercharge the entire food chain and increase biodiversity in our own small space, across the ocean, and on to other continents. Collectively, our gardens offer a more varied selection of plants in a small area compared to farmland and the surrounding countryside, producing the most nectar per unit area of land and the largest area of green land in UK cities – six times more than parks and 40 times more than allotments.[30]

Fill your garden with a wide range and the longest possible season of nectar- and pollen-rich plants (from a pesticide-free source), and reduce the area of lawn to leave more areas wild or allow lawn weeds to flower.

Pollinators also need water for drinking and a pond for breeding, as many have aquatic stages in their lifecycle. You can also provide nest sites for wild bees, beetles and bugs; they like bare soil along the base of trees and hedges, or even bird boxes.

WHY IT MATTERS
Global insect loss has been calculated at 2.5 per cent over the last 25–30 years. If this decline continues, in ten years we will have lost a quarter of all insects, in 50 years half and in 100 years we will have none.[31, 32]

Light pollution in coastal communities disrupts marine life

THE ISSUE

Marine species are extremely sensitive to light, and over millennia have evolved to respond to subtle cues from the natural cycles of seasonal light. Extensive lighting at night disrupts the ecosystems of marine organisms, leading to lower chances of survival and even bleaching of coral reefs.

....

WHAT CAN WE DO?

75 per cent of the world's megacities are coastal, and coastal populations are projected to more than double by 2060.[33] Wherever we live, we owe it to our local wildlife to think more carefully about our lighting. Only light areas where it's needed for safety, and avoid lighting up trees and water, which may be refuges or feeding grounds for nocturnal species.

A lot of artificial light is directed or reflected upwards and is clearly visible in space – use cones or baffle lights to direct the light to the ground and objects you need to see. White and blue LED lights, although more carbon efficient, are disruptive to wildlife – opt for warmer whites, red, and orange lights in your outside spaces. Switch off outside lights when you're not there – and avoid using fairy lights if you can.

If we spare a thought for our coastal habitats, urban wildlife, and nocturnal friends, we can save energy and money, and may even see some more stars and encourage wildlife to our gardens. It can help our own circadian rhythms too.

WHY IT MATTERS

Artificial lighting disrupts navigation, foraging, predation, breeding, and many other natural processes in our marine and terrestrial wildlife, and its use is increasing between 2–6 per cent per year globally.[34, 35]

Dogs can be a hazard to health and wildlife at the beach

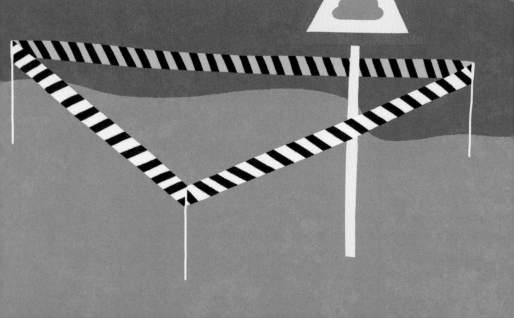

THE ISSUE

Dog poo is a growing problem on beaches – in the UK alone, beach cleans collected 792 bags of dog waste from 364 sites.[36] Dogs also pose a threat to wildlife, with the best habitats and the breeding season for beach-nesting shore birds overlapping with popular recreation sites and holiday periods.

WHAT CAN WE DO?

Always pick up your dog's mess and dispose of it – wherever you are. Never bury your dog's poo in the sand, assuming it will decay or be washed away (it won't), and never leave the bag hanging on a bush or hidden behind a stone – even a biodegradable bag will be there for the next three years and a compostable one for a year.[37]

Coastal managers have tried to combat the risks caused by dogs to wildlife at the beach by setting up no-dog zones and areas where dogs must be kept on the lead. Look out for these and make sure you comply – they may be to keep beaches and coastal waters clean during the main holiday season, or they may be to protect nesting shorebirds. Ground-dwelling birds are also vulnerable to direct attack from dogs, and are even disturbed by dogs on the lead.[38]

WHY IT MATTERS

The UK Environment Agency's testing of bathing water beaches showed that, at 42 of the 59 beaches with poor water quality, dog and bird poo contributed more than 10 per cent of the faecal contamination.[39]

94 per cent of fulmars in the North Sea have plastic in their gut[40]

THE ISSUE
Beach litter can be ingested by sea life, leading to injury and death. The total number of species impacted by marine litter stood at 817 in 2016, up 23 per cent from 2012.[41]

....

WHAT CAN WE DO?
We need to reduce the amount of rubbish littering our beaches and entering the sea. The most common items include plastic bottles, plastic bags, food packaging, cotton buds, cigarette butts, and wet wipes. If we reduce our use of these items, we take them out of the system.

When you buy food to eat on the go, choose recyclable packaging and make sure it finds its way to a recycling bin. If you bring food from home, always take it away with you once you're done.

Lobby local councils at beaches where you see accumulated rubbish and ask them to provide sufficient bin space. There are often just one or two food outlets creating the vast majority of the litter – have a word with them to see what they can do. It should be easy for people to remove their rubbish so that they have no excuse for littering.

Live by the philosophy of taking only memories and leaving only footprints. If you are active on social media, take pictures of rubbish that you find on the beach and tag it with #footprints to highlight the problem.

WHY IT MATTERS
Marine litter has been identified as having been ingested by at least 40 per cent of the world's seabird species, 100 per cent of turtle species, and 50 per cent of mammals. Evidence is also growing for ingestion by mussels and oysters, lugworms, shrimps, and zooplankton.[42]

Limited scientific information on our marine environment is hampering global marine conservation

THE ISSUE
Government funding for marine research is much less than that of other scientific fields. On average, countries commit only 1.7 per cent of their research budget to the ocean[43], hampering efforts to understand and develop strategies to protect it.

WHAT CAN WE DO?
Marine and coastal citizen science volunteering can provide opportunities for all of us to get involved in marine conservation-related investigations, such as monitoring reef systems, categorizing whale calls, and tracking marine debris. These studies can get you out with others and are even accessible from your home, with just online access required.

If you are able to get to the coast, you can get involved in beach cleans to identify and track the types of marine litter on our shoreline, or be trained up to identify and record marine life. Current online projects include exploring Sweden's marine biodiversity via deep-water video recordings, and identifying plankton species recorded on a continuous digital sampler. This data can then be analysed and used by decision-makers to understand changes.

WHY IT MATTERS
In 2019, 1 million volunteers from 122 countries took part in the International Coastal Clean-up[44], and almost 11,000 people took part in the Great British Beach Clean. Data from the latter event was used to lobby government on the need for a plastic bag levy; since the introduction of the 5p charge in north-western European countries, plastic bag litter on the sea bed of the North Sea has reduced by 30 per cent.[45]

Why is ocean warming such a big deal for our planet?

Concentrations of greenhouse gases are building up in our atmosphere, largely as a result of fossil fuel consumption. They are known as greenhouse gases as they cause the greenhouse effect: absorbing and re-radiating the sun's energy, warming the atmosphere and the surface of the earth.

The ocean absorbs huge quantities of the heat produced by the greenhouse effect. In fact, with its vast mass and high heat capacity, it acts as a buffer, protecting humans from much more rapid effects of climate change. The ocean has absorbed 93 per cent of the excess heat from greenhouse gases since the 1970s[46]; it has been estimated that if the same amount of heat absorbed in the top 2 kilometres of the ocean between 1955 and 2010 had gone into the lower 10 kilometres of atmosphere, the earth would have warmed by 36°C.[47]

Average global sea surface temperatures have increased by 0.13°C every decade for the last 100 years, and the deep ocean is also affected, with around a third of the excess heat being absorbed at more than 700 metres below the surface.[48]

The ocean does not warm up evenly across its entire range: ocean heatwaves occur, and currents move and mix the heat around. The greatest ocean warming has occurred in the southern hemisphere, as evidenced by the subsurface melting of the Antarctic ice shelves.

Why is it important?

Ocean warming comes with many side effects for climate, for biodiversity, and for humans. Warm water cannot hold as much of the oxygen as marine organisms need to survive. And the impact of deoxygenation as a result of ocean warming is exacerbated by ocean acidification – a decrease in pH caused by the absorption of CO_2 as the ocean buffers increasing CO_2 in the atmosphere. Ocean warming is already affecting marine species, prompting mass movement as they search for suitable environmental conditions; for those species with a limited range and ability to move, survival is already a challenge – many coastal ecosystems including coral reefs are clearly demonstrating increased mortality, and the outlook is bleak.

Warming water expands and ice melts, causing sea levels to rise. Along with the decline in coral reefs, mangroves, and seagrasses, which protect the coast from erosion, this exacerbates the problem for coastal communities and low-lying island countries such as those in the Pacific.[49]

Differential ocean warming is also changing the way water moves around the planet. Ocean circulation has a central role in regulating our climate patterns and supporting marine life through the movement of heat, nutrients, and oxygen. Global warming is weakening the movement of these currents, the consequences of which could be dramatic changes in weather patterns across the Atlantic and in western Europe, and disruption of fish populations and other marine life. It could ultimately lead to irreversible climatic impacts, the socio-economic consequences of which could be significant.

Community action is accelerating positive change to help our ocean

Our global ocean needs a global plan to bring it back from the edge of collapse. The climate crisis, overfishing, pollution and overexploitation of the seabed for minerals and oil have pushed the ocean to its limit. Scientists have concluded that a worldwide network of protected areas is the best solution to save our biggest ecosystem. The call is out for governments to sign up to protect 30 per cent of the ocean by 2030, and many are doing just that. And while government commitments are essential for global success, strong community ownership is essential for local success. There are many examples from around the world where communities are taking the lead in conserving their local marine ecosystems.

Puerto Morelos reef on the Yucatán Peninsula in Mexico is the dream holiday destination – long white beaches with a turquoise sea and the Mesoamerican Reef (the Western Hemisphere's largest barrier reef) just 400 metres offshore. But all was not right in paradise. Climate change, overfishing, and uncontrolled tourism and its associated pollution, along with direct impacts from snorkelling and diving, was destroying the reef system. A marine protected area (MPA) was created and the highly motivated and aware local community has managed this effectively, drawing in funds from tourists to keep the programme going. Community ownership has been a key factor in the success of this MPA.

Fiji's archipelagic state of islands is heavily dependent on its marine and coastal ecosystems for physical, economic, social, and cultural resources. Clams are a staple food for the villagers of Ucunivanua on the eastern coast of Fiji's largest island, and by the 1990s they were becoming hard to find. This signalled a decline in the community's marine resources and a wider pattern of resource depletion throughout Fiji. The community reacted by setting up a protected area. Seagrass and mudflats in front of the village were closed to clam harvesting for three years, building on the tradition of prohibitions for harvesting certain species. After seven years of local management, the clam populations had recovered, and village income had risen significantly. Word of the success of this first Local Marine Management Area (LMMA) spread and other villages and islands set up their own. The network has now grown to the extent that there are over 400 villages around Fiji with similarly protected areas.

The island of Kauai in Hawaii has the community of Ha'ena its north shore. The community has a strong identity and culture, and after 25 years of hard work and sustained pressure by the local non-profit group, Hui Maka'āinana o Makana, they persuaded the government to grant them permission to establish the first community-based Subsistence Fishing Area. Using their traditional ecological knowledge, they manage the nearshore fisheries, incorporating a sanctuary area (pu'uhonua) to protect their marine resources. The success of the scheme is being shared and plans for more community management across Hawaii are being developed.

Chapter 3

Transport

Sea bed mining, toxic waste, and a massive carbon footprint: the lifecycle of our cars is destroying the ocean

THE ISSUE
From manufacture to disposal, cars are depleting our natural resources, adding to the pollution load on the ocean and contributing to global carbon emissions.

....

WHAT CAN WE DO?
In England, around 60 per cent of 1–2 mile trips are made by car.[50] We could immediately reduce our personal carbon emissions by walking, cycling, scooting, or taking public transport for more of these short journeys – to school, to work, to the shops . . . And we may be able to survive without our own cars at all. Today, there are many alternatives to individual car ownership, particularly if you live in an urban setting.

For longer journeys or when you have lots of people or kit to transport, car sharing companies and initiatives have been set up in most big cities. Often mediated through apps, they allow you to use a car for a few hours or days, without the expense and hassle of owning your own. These schemes can reduce the number of cars needed and as a result have a big impact on emissions.[51]

And if there is poor transport provision in your area, campaign in your community for a dedicated bus service, improved cycling facilities, or car, bike, and scooter sharing clubs – and encourage people to use them.

WHY IT MATTERS
Over a car's lifespan, an estimated 10 per cent of its total carbon footprint comes from manufacture, 5 per cent from disposal, and the remaining 85 per cent during use.

Poor air quality kills 7 million people globally each year[52]

THE ISSUE

One of the biggest sources of greenhouse gases and air pollution is transport.[53] These emissions are killing off marine life and preventing the ocean from playing its essential role in regulating the global climate.

WHAT CAN WE DO?

Choosing to ride a bike will help save the ocean. It is also great for our health and cheaper than running a car: the cost of buying and maintaining a bike is around 1 per cent of the cost of buying and maintaining a car.[54] It also gives independence to those that cannot afford a car.

To get started, all you need is a bike and a helmet – try your local bike shop, or you can often find cheap second-hand bikes at garage sales, online recycling and trading sites, or if you have a workplace cycle scheme you may be able to get a grant to help you buy one.

Some places allow cycling on footpaths as long as you are mindful of pedestrians and give them right of way; alternatively, you will need to stick to dedicated cycle paths or roads. Cycling away from cars is much safer and avoids poor air quality, so have a search for specific cycle routes.

WHY IT MATTERS

Road transport contributes 70 per cent of nitrogen dioxide (NO_2) concentrations and 30 per cent of particulate matter in areas with poor air quality.[55]

Mining for rare earth metals used in electric vehicle batteries is destroying the ocean floor

THE ISSUE
While the move to electric vehicles (EVs) is essential to meet net zero and improve air quality, it comes at a cost. There are more rare earth metals accessible on the ocean floor than on land[56], but ocean mining has a devastating impact, destroying the sea bed and the biodiversity on it.

....

WHAT CAN WE DO?
EVs have considerably lower lifetime carbon emissions than internal combustion engine vehicles[57], and as we move increasingly to renewable sources of electricity, the balance moves further towards EVs and will only get stronger. Current EV batteries only last ten years and use rare earth metals such as cobalt, but the battery life is getting longer and the need for metal elements may be reduced as technologies change.

The financial considerations of buying an EV – the initial cost, its associated insurance, and installing charging points – add up to a big upfront outlay. But with low running and minimal maintenance costs, you – and the ocean – can expect to reap the benefits within three years.[58]

If you get an EV, remember that every journey still has a carbon footprint and your tyres are still producing microplastics that wash into the sea. Drive conservatively, reduce the number of journeys you make, and take care of the car and battery to make them last. At the end of life, make sure it is recycled and rare metals retrieved.

WHY IT MATTERS
Meeting just the UK's targets for electric cars by 2050 would require nearly twice the world's current output of cobalt. Whatever is in the path of mining machines will be destroyed, and the plumes of silt and sand churned up will endanger marine life far beyond the mining site.[59]

Tyre dust is the second largest source of microplastics in our ocean[60]

THE ISSUE
Car tyre wear and tear contributes as much ocean microplastic pollution as plastic bottles, bags, and microfibres from clothing combined. These plastics are ingested by marine life, impacting the health of marine species and ultimately ending up in our food.

....

WHAT CAN WE DO?
The choices we make about our cars and the way we drive and maintain our vehicles can make a huge difference to the impact of tyre wear and tear on local air quality and microplastic pollution in the ocean.

Drive gently and watch your speed. Driving fast, with racing starts, sudden stops, and sharp cornering increases tyre damage. At around 50mph, dust production will be lowest, rising dramatically above 70mph.

Tyre and road wear increase with the weight of vehicles, so go for the smallest car you can get away with to reduce particulate emissions. And try to lighten up accessories and luggage – roof racks and boxes, cycle racks, and unnecessary kit in the boot add drag and weight, increasing tyre friction on the road.

Make sure you keep your car in good working order. Regular servicing and making sure tyres are kept at the correct pressure helps keep your car efficient and can reduce tyre wear and tear.

WHY IT MATTERS
Car tyre wear and tear is estimated to contribute between 5 and 10 per cent of all ocean plastics and, according to the IUCN, up to 28 per cent of all microplastics entering our oceans each year.[61, 62]

Greenhouse gases released by air travel are depriving our oceans of oxygen

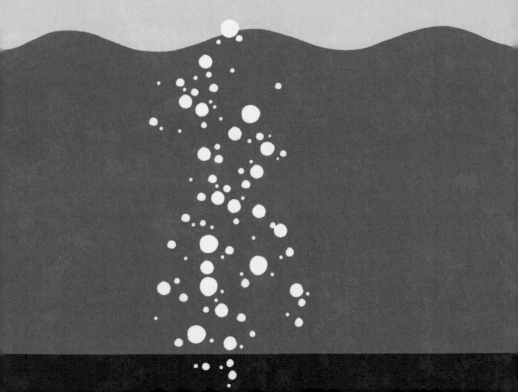

THE ISSUE

More than 90 per cent of the energy trapped by greenhouse gases in our atmosphere is absorbed by the oceans, causing ocean warming and deoxygenation of already oxygen-poor deep ocean areas. Air travel emits greenhouse gases directly into the upper atmosphere, causing more damage than those released at ground level.[63]

....

WHAT CAN WE DO?

To fly or not to fly is one of the most greenhouse-gas-intensive choices we make, and a real opportunity to take personal action: one less flight a year could reduce our emissions by up to 50 per cent.

For a personal holiday, try replacing a flight with train travel. Taking the train from London to Paris rather than flying cuts carbon emissions by 90 per cent; it can even be quicker door to door.[64] And there are now so many digital options that it makes both economic and environmental sense for technological solutions to take the place of long-haul flights for businesses. Even travelling by car can be more climate friendly: travelling solo has similar carbon emissions to flying, but each additional passenger increases the carbon efficiency.

If you do need to fly, look for airlines with newer, more energy-efficient aircraft, and take just one flight rather than hopping your way around the world, as emissions are greatest during take off and landing.

WHY IT MATTERS

Aviation accounts for up to 75 per cent of the tourism industry's greenhouse gas emissions.[65]

Why is ocean mining such a concern for our deep-sea ecosystems?

Recent discoveries of mineral deposits (such as polymetallic nodules and cobalt-rich ferromanganese crusts) in the deep sea, along with the rise in demand for their use in electric vehicle batteries and other high-tech industries are fuelling the interest in deep-sea-bed mining.

None of the technology being developed for extraction is focused on protecting the pristine deep ocean environment. Direct impacts of mining result from the physical removal of the mineral deposits, which kills the resident biota as well as destroying the habitat, fragmenting and isolating other species and habitats, and disrupting sediment dynamics and chemistry. Deep sea sediments rich in methanogenic microbes are important in the sequestration of methane, and their loss or disturbance could have implications for the climate. Indirect environmental impacts, in the vicinity of the mined area and beyond, are poorly understood and hard to predict, but are likely to include smothering of habitats and species by sediment plumes and the release of nutrient-rich and toxin-laden water into sensitive deep-sea ecosystems.

Companies rushing to establish rights and gain exploration licences at the same time as governments are negotiating to establish protection for biodiversity in the high seas, is creating an increasingly fraught geopolitical issue.

Why is it important?

The deep sea is our planet's last pristine environment – vast and unexplored, it has had fewer human visitors than the highest mountains and remotest corners of our terrestrial world. The biodiversity of the deep ocean, although little studied, is known to be rich and dynamic and a fundamental cog in the processes of global carbon cycles and climate regulation. Typically, deposits of rare minerals are often associated with sea bed features such as hydrothermal vents and seamounts, which are key locations for exceptionally rich and specialized biodiversity.

Some believe that deep sea minerals are essential for our decarbonized future, but mining has the potential to disrupt 'blue carbon', which aims to maximize the carbon sequestration potential of the ocean. If we do not proceed carefully, deep-sea mining could exacerbate both climate change and biodiversity crises. And the impacts are likely to be irreversible.

Given the limited knowledge of our deep-sea environments, the rapid pace at which the industry is developing, and the potential for adverse impacts, many environmentalists, including Sir David Attenborough, and governments are calling for a moratorium on deep-sea mining in the short term. They say we should not rush to mine this pristine and unexplored environment, risking devastating and irreversible impacts, until we have better science on which to base our decisions. Consideration should also be given to other sources of minerals, for example through untapped recycling potential, as well as other technologies that are not dependent on metals.

Alternative energy solutions in the ocean can help end our reliance on fossil fuels

There is a vast store of energy waiting to be exploited in the ocean. Wind, waves, and currents combined account for 300 times more energy than we currently use; almost 90 per cent of global wind energy is contained in the turbulence above the world's oceans. Despite restrictions needed to protect areas for shipping and fishing access, as well as environmentally sensitive areas, there is a huge untapped resource waiting to be harnessed to deliver a significant share of our global energy needs.

For many years the vast majority of our renewable energy has been sourced on the land, but the offshore renewable energy tide is turning and there are other technologies under development in the six main marine renewable energies:

Offshore wind is the most advanced offshore renewable energy source. Many wind projects are already operational, many concentrated in the shallow waters of the continental shelf around Europe. Facilities are getting bigger all the time and moving further offshore into deeper waters and on floating platforms, which opens up opportunities at many more locations worldwide.

There are various technical concepts that convert wave energy to electricity, all of which use the up-down motion of a device floating in the ocean to drive turbines. The total projected generating potential of wave power would deliver 10 per cent of global energy needs. However, to date, the promise has not been fulfilled. Few projects have progressed beyond prototype or pilot, but investment allowing more commercial-scale development may be increasing again as climate change pressures increase.

Tidal energy can exploit the kinetic energy present in the horizontal movement of water in the ebb and flow phases of tidal flow, using much the same concept that onshore hydropower does using downhill flow of water under gravity. Alternatively, tidal energy can also use the potential energy in the difference in height between the high and low tides captured behind an ocean-based barrage or dam. Tidal energy has been used commercially in a handful of locations and on a small scale for several years, but concerns about the environmental damage of barrage schemes has prevented significant scale-up worldwide, and alternatives exploiting kinetic energy have been the focus of development in recent years.

Ocean currents hold vast stores of energy which can drive submerged turbines. A number of prototypes have been developed and tested based on wind turbine technology – the stresses and strains they are subjected to in the water is the challenge that must be overcome in realizing the huge potential for renewable energy supply from ocean currents.

Ocean Thermal Energy Conversion (OTEC) exploits temperature differences between warm surface water and cold deep water to generate power. Temperature differences must be in excess of 20°C, so this is suitable for warmer marine areas. Initially considered uneconomic, recent progress and investment in the technology has picked up.

Osmotic power plants exploit the osmotic pressure that builds up between saltwater and freshwater when they are pumped into a double chamber separated by a semi-permeable membrane. This technology is still in its infancy, with lots of potential for future development.

Other than offshore wind power, these technologies are still in early stages of development, requiring government subsidies and investment to undertake prototype scale trails. The next stage of development, where they may attract commercial investment, is just taking off.

Chapter 4

On Holiday

Tourists produce four times the amount of plastic waste than they would at home

THE ISSUE

Over the summer months, holiday-makers cause a huge surge in marine litter, most of which is plastic waste, typically: drink bottles, food packaging, inflatable toys, plastic holiday gifts, and polystyrene bodyboards.

....

WHAT CAN WE DO?

Take your conscientious and ethical mind with you when you go on holiday: continue to think about disposing of food packaging responsibly, take a refillable drinks bottle, a reusable shopping bag, and refuse plastic stirrers and straws in cocktails.

If you want to enjoy the surf, don't be tempted by cheap bodyboards wrapped in nylon, many of which are discarded after a week, or left to float out to sea. Before they even get to the surf they have exerted a massive carbon footprint – manufactured from plastic in China and transported around the world. If you want to body board, hire one or buy a more expensive, durable one – it makes financial sense in the long run.

Pack plastic-free toiletries and use reusable packing cubes or cloth bags rather than plastic bags to organize your packing.

WHY IT MATTERS

200 million tourists visit the Mediterranean each year, causing a 40 per cent surge in marine litter over the summer months. The Mediterranean holds 1 per cent of the world's seawater but 7 per cent of the worlds microplastic waste.[66]

14,000 tons of toxic sunscreen washes into the sea each year[67]

THE ISSUE
The UV-filtering compounds found in sunscreen products wash off our skin in the sea, and shower and have toxic effects on coral reefs and other marine organisms.[68]

....

WHAT CAN WE DO?
Skin cancer is a very real risk, so it is important that we protect ourselves from the sun. However, we can do this without resorting to ocean-damaging sprays. Search out shade between 10am and 2pm – the hottest part of the day – under a tree, umbrella, or sunshade. Cover up with UV protective clothing and slap on a pair of sunglasses and a hat.

When you buy a sunscreen, make sure it is ocean friendly. The Protect Land + Sea certification is reliable, but be wary of those that claim to be 'reef safe' or 'biodegradable' as they don't always cut out the most harmful chemicals. Avoid ingredients that can harm marine life, such as: oxybenzone, benzophenone-1, benzophenone-8, OD-PABA, 4-methylbenzylidene camphor, 3-benzylidene camphor, nano-titanium dioxide, nano-zinc oxide, octinoxate, octocrylene.[69]

Think about how you apply your sunscreen – sprays tend to end up all over the sand and rocks around you, which increases the load in the water. Use a cream rather than a spray.

WHY IT MATTERS
Covering just 0.1 per cent of the ocean floor, coral reefs support 25 per cent of marine species, and provide us with food, coastal protection, and tourism. Yet 70–90 per cent of these precious ecosystems are projected to be lost by 2050 if we don't take action.

Picturesque tourism and social media are driving coastal destinations to destruction

THE ISSUE
Tourism puts a huge strain on fragile coastal ecosystems[70], resulting in the erosion of coastal paths and cliffs, increased pollution, effluent discharge into the sea, and escalating pressure on endangered species.[71, 72]

....

WHAT CAN WE DO?
We can be a little lazy when it comes to holidays, opting for places we can get to easily, or that we have seen and loved on someone's social media feed. Once there, we rush around ticking our own photo opportunity boxes, adding to the overcrowding of small areas and overloading the local infrastructure, leading to degradation of the local environment.

Search out the routes less travelled, and where possible travel out of season. Once you are there, spend a little more time in each place rather than rushing around from one overvisited sight to another. This will allow you to immerse yourself in the local environment and way of life and find quieter places to explore off the beaten track – probably only a scant few miles from the packed and crowded places that everyone else is visiting.

Travelling independently also allows money to trickle down into the local economy rather than sustaining the big tour operators.

Some travel companies specialize in sustainable or responsible travel, sourcing holiday destinations that help the local community and enhance the environment of travel destinations. These are a great place to start.

WHY IT MATTERS
In the UK alone, coastal margin habitats have declined in total area by around 10 per cent due to tourism development.[73]

Poorly managed coastal tourism industries are devastating marine life

THE ISSUE

The vast quantities of coral, shells, and other marine life collected for holiday souvenirs fuel an illegal trade generating $23 billion a year. Meanwhile, whale and dolphin watching is estimated to have an annual turnover of $2 billion, attracting 13 million people a year.[74, 75]

....

WHAT CAN WE DO?

Choose your tour operator carefully. While some tours can be hugely damaging to marine species and their associated ecosystems, well-managed experiences conducted by an informed guide provide opportunities for research, conservation, and environmental education. You can assess a company's credentials by checking their website or asking questions of the staff. Look out for tour operators and accommodation displaying the Global Sustainable Tourism Council (GSTC) logo, and check they adhere to the best practice guidelines for cetacean, shark, and turtle watching.[76]

When you are shopping for souvenirs, don't be tempted by shells, coral jewellery, turtle-shell, sea urchins, or pufferfish. Souvenirs harvested from the ocean can disrupt the balance of life and remove vital elements that ecosystems need to survive. And don't buy plastic tat – these are not made locally, so only a small percentage is going to the local population. Go for locally crafted gifts that reflect the area's heritage, supporting the existing way of life rather than encouraging changes to meet the tourist need.

WHY IT MATTERS

An estimated 14–30 million fish, 1.5 million live stony corals, and 9–10 million other invertebrates are removed each year from marine ecosystems across the world to supply the aquarium, home décor, and coral jewellery industries.[77]

What is the significance of human activities changing ocean soundscapes?

Sound travels further and faster in water than in air, and as a result many marine animals rely on it for communication as well as interpretation of their environment. Human activity is having a significant impact on the marine soundscape, creating an acoustic fog, changing the ocean environment, and threatening important behaviours in marine organisms.

Man-made noise – anthrophony – is increasing. Over the past 50 years, shipping has increased low-frequency noise on major routes by 32 times.[78] Fishing vessels use sonar to find shoals of fish, and bottom trawlers rumble across the sea bed. Oil rig construction, coastal development and offshore wind farms bang pile drivers into the sea bed and whirr away day and night. Resource exploration uses seismic booms to gather information about oil and mineral resources available in the ocean floor.

Noise made by natural processes – geophony – has been altered by climate change. The pattern of storms and sea ice movement change the soundscape, as does increased acidification of the ocean, which means sound travels even further, making the ocean even noisier. Meanwhile, the biophony – sounds of biological origin – has reduced as populations of sound-making animals decline due to overfishing and habitat degradation.

We have fundamentally altered the soundscape of our ocean since pre-industrial times, and it is having an impact on marine life.

Why is it important?

Sound is the sense that marine animals rely on most, as it travels furthest through the water column. From the smallest marine invertebrates to the largest whales, marine life interprets and explores its environment through sound, as well as communicating within and between species. Sound is used to catch prey, navigate, defend territory, and attract mates, as well as find homes and warn of attack.

We know that whales communicate over long distances. Sperm whales and some dolphins and porpoises use sonar to echolocate prey, while the humpback whale song has regional dialects and baleen whale calls can travel across ocean basins. Evidence shows that whales that used to travel throughout the ocean, staying in contact over hundreds of miles, are now restricted to staying within ten miles of each other to be able to communicate. And there are many other animals that rely on sound to communicate and reproduce: for example, the male toadfish hums to attract its mate, and cod produce thumps and growls with their swim bladder to encourage females to release their eggs.

There is clear evidence that the noise we produce from boats, sonar, energy and construction infrastructure, and seismic surveys limits the ability of animals to hear the natural soundscape of their environment, which induces physiological and behavioural changes.

The great news is that noise pollution, unlike most other human damage to the environment, is rapidly reversible. Removing the noise source removes the stressor, allowing marine animals to reverse their behaviour changes and return to their old habits.

Ecotourism contributing to marine conservation

Ecotourism is a form of responsible travel that connects people with the natural world to support conservation of the environment and the wellbeing of the local community.

Critics of ocean ecotourism have raised concerns over the impact of visitors on marine species. Reduced visitor numbers during Covid-19 appeared to improveconditions for marine wildlife, with associated changes in behaviour and distribution of some marine mammals and other species. Cynics also raise concerns of greenwashing, accusing ecotourism operators of environmentally destructive practices that they hide behind businesses marketed as eco friendly.

Nevertheless, significant evidence points to the positive benefits of ecotourism on local communities, local marine environments, visitors, and the wider environmental stewardship. If they are well-managed, they provide a revenue stream for marine protected areas and related conservation initiatives, stimulate a sustainable tourism economy with opportunities and income for local communities and local fishermen, ensure the protection of target marine habitats and species, and build environmental awareness through an educational experience.

Examples of marine ecotourism holidays include:

Marine conservation on a Thai island – working with full-time staff to protect Thailand's fragile reef ecology and developing conservation skills. Tasks might include reef predator management, reef surveys, sea turtle release, water testing, and beach cleans – and getting a diving certificate.

Swimming with whale sharks in the Philippines – the equivalent of going on an African safari to see terrestrial apex predators such as lions. As a result of ecotourism, sharks are now worth more alive than they are dead: an individual live reef shark is worth $250,000 in dive tourism, compared to $50 when dead. A study into the attitudes of local fishermen and shark hunters showed that having previously hunted whale sharks, they now protect them, actively encouraging others to care for the ocean and to use more sustainable fishing practices.

Whale conservation in the Azores – assisting a team of biologists to collect photo-ID and ecological data on both blue and sperm whales. Volunteers gain knowledge and experience of cetacean biology, conservation, and identification at sea and from land-based lookouts, help to collect and catalogue research data, and educate and support whale-watching visitors.

Turtle conservation in Greece – helping to protect breeding sea turtles on the coast with such roles as morning surveys, nest shading and protection, public awareness and education, beach cleans, and beach patrols.

It is clear that marine ecotourism has a role in conserving marine ecosystems in the same way that wildlife watching and volunteering holidays in bird reserves, national parks, and game parks does in terrestrial conservation.

Chapter 5

At Work

A 'use and throw' approach to office equipment is depleting marine resources faster than they can be replenished

THE ISSUE
We can no longer sustain a linear take, make, waste economy – we must change our mindset and see waste as a design flaw to be eliminated. Computer equipment is a particular problem and one of the world's fastest growing waste streams.

....

WHAT CAN WE DO?
We need to design waste and pollution out of how we operate our workplaces as well as our manufacturing processes. The outcome is a circular economy where waste streams become valuable resources – redirected back into manufacture rather than dumped in landfill.

All businesses have a corporate environmental responsibility and should be taking action – understanding and measuring climate and nature-related risks and opportunities, and committing to net zero carbon and nature-positive pathways.

Reporting on environmental responsibility is an important step so businesses can demonstrate the progress they are making in comparison to their peers. It also allows consumers, investors, and potential employees to invest in those companies that are doing the 'right' thing. If the company you work for is not performing well, then find out why. And if you are the person to ask – take action.

WHY IT MATTERS
A circular economy could result in $700 million annual material cost savings in the fast-moving consumer goods industry, and lead to a 48 per cent reduction in CO2 emissions by 2030.[79]

Driving to work increases your carbon footprint from fuel consumption, and working from home is not always working for our oceans

THE ISSUE
Greenhouse gas emissions caused by the peak-time traffic commute are putting a strain on our ocean, but heating and cooling individual home offices also has a huge carbon footprint.

WHAT CAN WE DO?
To make home working more ocean friendly, move to a renewable energy supplier or install solar panels. A 'smart' meter shows energy use in real-time and allows you to heat rooms differentially, encouraging more sustainable energy use. Cut out any draughts and sort out your insulation. Working from home also makes it easier to prepare your own food and drinks, in turn cutting down on packaged food and coffee.

Alternatively, greening the commute isn't as hard as you might think. If you drive an average car to work, then taking the bus, riding a motorcycle, or moving to electric will reduce your emissions. Check out car pool options in your neighbourhood, or think about going on foot or bike.

Where you live in the world, or even just the different seasons, can have an impact. If you require little or no heating but have a long commute, then working from home will have a much lower carbon footprint. If you are dependent on heating or air con at home and your commute is short, then it is almost certainly more carbon-efficient to go to the office.

WHY IT MATTERS
In the UK, working from home in summer saves around 400 kilograms of carbon emissions, the equivalent of 5 per cent of a typical British commuter's annual carbon footprint. However, working from home all year round would produce 2.5 tonnes of carbon per year – around 80 per cent more than an office worker.[80]

THE ISSUE
Pensions are supposed to ensure that we have a secure future, so investing in funds that finance fossil fuel extraction, putting us on the track to catastrophic climate meltdown, is illogical in the extreme.

WHAT CAN WE DO?
Workplace pensions are set up by your employer. Traditionally, these rarely had strong environmental credentials, but a good employer will now be investing ethically. If not, you have the ability to decide where to invest your money; a personal pension gives you full flexibility to craft your own product. Consumer finance websites and independent advisors produce lists of ethical investors based on extensive due diligence.

Be alert to 'greenwashing', when companies try to win your business with claims that appeal to your values – a company may be digging up fossil fuels at the same time as making its vehicle fleet electric.

Some providers charge slightly more to invest in ESG (environmental, social and governance) aligned funds to cover the due diligence required, so shop around. You can be confident you are not sacrificing returns for your ethical investments, however – recent studies have shown that sustainable funds have done better than non-ESG funds over the last one, five, and ten years.[81] And by investing in these, you will be part of the solution, encouraging other parts of the industry to follow suit.

WHY IT MATTERS
Moving a £100,000 pension pot invested in a traditional portfolio with oil and gas companies to a positive impact portfolio is the equivalent of taking five or six cars off the road a year.[82]

What is the significance of biodiversity loss in the ocean?

The ocean is home to millions of species, supporting a greater biodiversity than the land. Long-term patterns show that marine biodiversity cycles through periods of slow increase with occasional mass extinctions.

Post-industrialization, our ocean has been under pressure from human activities; climate change is leading to rising temperatures, ocean acidification, and extreme climatic events; while overfishing, dredging, mining, and eutrophication from nutrient pollution pile on the pressure and make it hard for species and systems to adapt.

The outcome has been measured in species extinctions, declining abundance and changing population structures. From phytoplankton, the primary producers forming the base of the food chain, through to the marine mammals and seabirds at the apex, scientists are observing changing patterns of abundance, distribution, and activity; where species are seen, how many of them, and when they are there is changing fast.

Species need to be able to adapt to the new conditions or migrate to areas which suit their needs. When change is too fast, species that can't move or adapt quickly enough disappear – as seen with coral reefs.

The full picture of biodiversity change and loss in global waters is hampered by the small fraction of species in the deep seas and polar oceans that have been identified. Nevertheless, evidence suggests that marine biological diversity is declining more rapidly than ever before in the earth's history.

Why is it important?

We rely on the ocean's biodiversity for the many services it provides in terms of food, resilience to climate change, nutrient cycling, climate regulation, coastal protection, raw materials, leisure and recreation, and cultural heritage.

Losing marine biodiversity weakens marine ecosystems. As we lose diversity in any system, we reduce its resilience; in the case of the ocean, this presents as being increasingly sensitive to climate change and losing its ability to deliver its crucial roles as ecological and climate regulator. The health of the ocean depends on the variety of life that it sustains, and our life on this planet is dependent on a healthy ocean.

We have so much to learn about our relatively unexplored marine environment. We have ravaged the land and reached beyond its limits, and we need to learn from this and treat our oceans and seas with respect. Current research is discovering novel antibacterial molecules from seaweeds that may be developed into much-needed new antibiotic agents. Other medical and technological advances may rely on our learning from organisms and habitats we have yet to even discover. There are many unknowns about the resources and potential the ocean has to help us adapt and live in our future, responding to our changing world.

Heroes: Ocean-friendly business

Many businesses are taking action to restore important marine habitats. Here are three exciting examples:

Sky set up Sky Ocean Rescue in 2017 to make people aware of plastic pollution and provide ideas for easy ways for all of us to take action, every day. So far, their campaign for change has reached nearly 48 million people across Europe. Working with the World Wide Fund for Nature (WWF) and research institutions, they have launched Seagrass Ocean Rescue. They are restoring seagrass in collaboration with the local community in Dale, West Wales, as a trial and plan to inspire future projects in other areas to restore the UK's seagrass meadows.

Seagrass is one of the least protected ecosystems on the planet. As much as 92 per cent of UK seagrass has been lost, along with the ocean health benefits it provides. Seagrass supports 30 times more biodiversity than neighbouring habitats; 20 per cent of juveniles in the world's fisheries use it as nurseries; and it sequesters more than 25 times as much carbon as rainforests. It also protects our coasts by dissipating wave energy and filtering pollution.

Coral reefs cover 0.1 per cent of the ocean floor but support 25 per cent of marine species. They are teetering on the edge of extinction as a result of climate change and mismanagement, and although they can adapt and recover naturally, the predicted rate of ocean warming is likely to outpace recovery. Without help, 70–90 per cent are projected to disappear by 2050.

Mars, working with marine scientists and local reef communities, have developed the Mars Assisted Reef Restoration System (MARRS). This consists of small steel frames (reef stars) to which rescued or nursery grown coral fragments are attached. These reef stars can be fixed together by divers on damaged coral reefs, forming a stable interconnected structure which supports dramatic growth and good survival rates. Over the past decade, dive teams have installed almost 20,000 reef stars using 290,000 coral fragments. These are already kick-starting natural recruitment, where new coral species are attracted to the restored reefs, providing new habitats for fish species.

Bycatch from commercial fishing is responsible for the deaths of over 300,000 dolphins, porpoises and whales, 300,000 seabirds and 250,000 turtles every year.[83] Death in fishing gear due to entanglement is the leading threat to the 80-plus species of whales, dolphins and porpoises in our ocean.

Triodos, a world leader in sustainable banking, has set up a crowdfunding platform where individuals can invest directly in pioneering organizations delivering positive change. One organization seeking funding is Fishtek Marine. Pioneers in marine conservation technology, they are seeking to raise equity to help with the sale and marketing of products aimed at the global commercial fishing industry, designed to deter the unintentional death or capture of non-target marine species, known as bycatch.

Chapter 6

Food & Shopping

The average European household throws away 25 per cent of its food

THE ISSUE
Global greenhouse gas emissions from food waste account for 8–10 per cent of total global GHG emissions (more than double the aviation industry), contributing to ocean warming.[84]

WHAT CAN WE DO?
Domestic food waste in the UK accounts for 70 per cent of the national annual food waste mountain. Yet we've already shown that we can reduce this: in the Covid-19 pandemic, as a result of more targeted shopping, monthly food waste in London reduced by 22 per cent.[85]

We need to start by making sure we do not buy too much food. Before going shopping, plan meals and only buy what's needed.

Then we need to eat what we buy. Cook in bulk and freeze in batches, and have a 'leftovers' night to finish up any extra bits.

Watch what you throw out – meat and dairy products have much higher carbon emissions than fruit and vegetables; a study in Swedish supermarkets showed that while fruit and veg made up 85 per cent of waste by weight, it only accounted for 46 per cent of greenhouse gas emissions, while meat was only 3.5 per cent of the waste but accounted for 29 per cent of emissions.[86]

Ideally, compost your food waste, use your curb-side food waste bin, or give your scraps to pets. One study estimated that the greenhouse gas emissions from composting are just 14 per cent of the same food waste sent to landfill.[87]

WHY IT MATTERS
Globally, 30 per cent of the food we produce is wasted.[88]

Overfishing and poor fishing practices are destroying marine ecosystems and fish stocks

THE ISSUE

Overfishing has pushed two-thirds of all marine fish stocks to their limit (and a third beyond sustainable levels)[89], bottom trawling is ploughing up habitats on the ocean floor, shrimp farming is destroying coastal mangroves[90], and fishing litter such as rope and nets makes up half of the total litter recorded in the open ocean.[91, 92]

WHAT CAN WE DO?

Consumer power can save our fish and marine ecosystems: buying only sustainably sourced fish sends a strong message through the supply chain. The challenge is knowing how to find sustainable fish.

When you buy fish and seafood, look for the Marine Stewardship Council (MSC) blue fish label. The MSC assesses fisheries on the basis of the impact they are having on wild fish populations and their marine ecosystems.[93] Although no certification system is perfect, they provide the best information available.

Avoid intensively farmed seafood, as there are concerns around animal welfare; the large quantities of fish food sourced from wild fish stocks or land-based soy; localized habitat destruction; nutrient and chemical pollution; as well as the potential for escapees' impact on wild fish stocks.

WHY IT MATTERS

Mangroves are nurseries for wild fish stocks, sources of wood for building, serve as buffers to storm surges, absorb carbon dioxide, and help counteract the effects of rising sea levels. A fifth of mangroves worldwide have been lost since 1980, mostly because of clearance to make way for shrimp farms, which then pollute the area with waste, antibiotics, and fertilizers.[94]

Transporting food around the world has a huge carbon footprint and disrupts marine life

THE ISSUE
Transport currently accounts for around 10 per cent of the carbon emissions of our food. While air freight emits around 50 times more per tons transported than sea freight,[95] the increase in cargo ship traffic threatens marine ecosystems, and busy shipping routes physically threaten marine mammals and turtles, as well as creating noise and light pollution.

....

WHAT CAN WE DO?
Air freighted food has a huge carbon footprint, and should be avoided. It can be hard to tell if food has been transported by air, however air travel is expensive so is only viable for high value, highly perishable food that needs to be eaten soon after harvesting – based on the product and the country of origin marked on labels, you should be able to work it out.

To reduce the reliance on sea freight, focus on choosing seasonal produce that can be grown locally; don't be tempted by local food grown out of season as the need for carbon-hungry greenhousing can actually result in higher emissions than transporting from overseas.

Ideally, buy as much of your food from local producers, farmers' markets, veg box companies, and other trusted suppliers of low-impact produce.

Consider highly perishable fresh fruit and veg as a seasonal treat or use your freezer rather than resorting to air freighted produce. Even better, if you can, grow your own seasonal produce.

WHY IT MATTERS
Transporting food to and around the UK produces 19 million tons of CO_2 annually – equivalent to around 5.5 million typical cars.[96]

Plastics from food and drink packaging dominate ocean litter

THE ISSUE
Of the top ten items of ocean litter, plastic bags, plastic bottles, food containers and cutlery, wrappers, container caps, and lids are all on the list.[97, 98] These are now contaminating even the most remote and deepest parts of the ocean.[99]

WHAT CAN WE DO?
We must stop this pollution at its source, using our consumer power to support zero waste supermarkets and food outlets that minimize the packaging around their food and cut out plastic options. And if your favourite shop or takeaway hasn't found their way to reducing their plastic packaging, have a word with them – and tell your friends to.

Whenever we do end up with food packaging, we can make sure we bin it responsibly and recycle where we can. Supermarkets and takeaways can help by having adequate recycling and waste disposal facilities on site.

Parks, visitor centres, and urban areas usually have a few green spaces which attract littering. If you notice food packaging accumulating in areas regularly, a bit of gentle lobbying of the local council to provide some bins may be all that is required; if they need more convincing, a community litter pick may be effective. Categorize the litter based on the shop it comes from as this provides hard evidence on the impact of individual shops and you can then raise the issue with them directly.

WHY IT MATTERS
A plastic drinks bottle left on the beach can last more than 450 years in the marine environment.[100]

Meat, dairy, and fish farming are polluting coastal waters

THE ISSUE

Fertilizers from arable crops, along with effluent from meat, dairy, and fish farming, add huge loads of nitrates and phosphates to our coastal waters, causing algal blooms which use up oxygen, leading to more than 500 marine 'dead zones' around the world.[101]

WHAT CAN WE DO?

Ruminant livestock, such as cattle and lamb, have by far the highest climate impact because they produce methane in their digestive system. They also produce large quantities of waste, which pollutes our water environment. Reducing meat, farmed fish, and dairy in our diets will help dramatically with nitrate, chemical, and pesticide pollution levels in coastal environments, as well as greenhouse gas emissions from meat and dairy. A recent study found that reducing the consumption of meat, dairy, and eggs in the EU by half could reduce nitrate emissions to groundwater and surface water by 40 per cent.[102] This shift in diet – with an accompanying increase in the consumption of organic, locally produced food – would reduce emissions by 25–40 per cent and also benefit our health.

In addition, organic and regenerative farming practices have been shown to reduce nutrient run-off through lower nitrogen application, better rotation with leguminous plants that fix nitrogen into the soil, and a move to practices that improve soil quality and reduce erosion.[103]

WHY IT MATTERS

Livestock accounts for around 18 per cent of global greenhouse gas emissions[104], and 78 per cent of global ocean and freshwater pollution is caused by agriculture.[105]

Chemicals used in agriculture are killing our coastal ecosystems – and can also end up on our plate

THE ISSUE

The seagrasses, coral reefs, and mangroves that fringe our coastlines – storing large quantities of carbon and providing natural sea defences for our coastal communities – are in danger of being wiped out by chemicals used in agriculture.[106, 107]

WHAT CAN WE DO?

Inherently toxic herbicides and pesticides spread in the environment by farmers are designed to have limited impact on non-target species, however they have not been well designed for the marine environment.

To avoid food farmed using pesticides, look out for organic-certified food, such as the Soil Association certification and organic green leaf badge of the EU. There may be slightly different regulations in different parts of the world, but you can be pretty certain that considerably fewer pesticides have been used in the production of these foods.

The additional cost of organic produce can be offputting, but if you sign up to a box scheme or shop at farmers' markets or farm shops, organic can be at least as cheap as the non-organic equivalents. Or consider prioritizing a few organic items and opt for some staples such as flour, milk, bread, and butter that can be cheaper or close in price to non-organic. And if you can't buy organic, the World Health Organization notes that consumers can limit their intake of pesticide residues by peeling or washing fruit and vegetables.[108]

WHY IT MATTERS

Large scale mortality of corals in the last 30 years has been well documented, along with 30–50 per cent losses of mangroves in the last 50 years[109] and almost 30 per cent of seagrass lost in the last decade.[110]

We are living beyond our planet's means and will destroy our ocean if we don't change

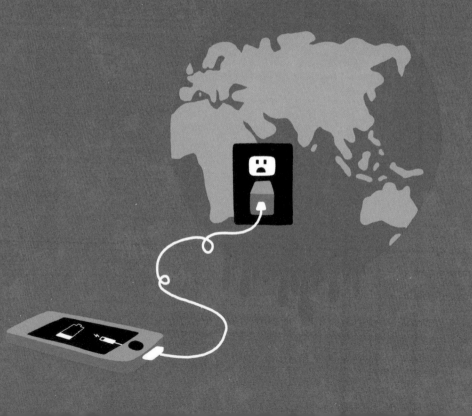

THE ISSUE

Our ocean is a finite resource, and we are outstripping supply in every area of our interaction. As a result, we are exceeding our ocean budget.

....

WHAT CAN WE DO?

The truth is that if we live a little differently, there is space and resource for all of us. It just needs a slight philosophical shift.

What really matters in our lives? Is it our iPad, or something else? Some things' we cannot do without, but many we can. Resist consumerism. If we buy only those things we actually 'need' rather than the things we are tempted by in adverts, we'd save ourselves a lot of money and waste. So, unsubscribe from email alerts, walk past billboards, turn over TV channels and flick past magazine adverts. And while you are at it, think critically about other external influences – friends, music, social media. Consumerism creeps in everywhere.

When something gets broken or begins to look a bit tatty, investigate how to mend it or renovate it rather than throwing it away and starting again – and if you can't reuse it, donate or sell it on.

Every time you go to throw something out or buy something new, think about the resources. Where did the raw materials for this 'thing' come from, what went into its production? Even the most seemingly inconsequential item – from a lettuce leaf to a pen – leaves a trail of impacts on people and the environment.

WHY IT MATTERS

Collectively, we have failed to manage our global portfolio of assets sustainably. Between 1992 and 2014, produced capital per person doubled, while the stock of natural capital per person declined by nearly 40 per cent.[111]

What are the impacts of ocean trawling?

Trawling is a method of fishing that involves dragging a heavy weighted net across the sea bed to catch fish. Large industrial fisheries favour bottom trawling as it can catch large quantities of fish in one go. Studies of satellite information from industrial trawlers between 2016 and 2019 suggest that 4.9 million km^2 or 1.3 per cent of the global ocean is trawled each year.[112]

One problem with bottom trawling is the indiscriminate nature of its activities. Much of the marine life captured is not commercially viable and is returned dead and damaged to the sea. Known as bycatch, this can include turtles, juvenile fish, invertebrates, and deep-sea corals, and depletes the non-target species as much as the targeted species. The weighted nets cause destruction of whole habitats and associated ecosystems, much like bulldozing ancient forests on land. Sea mounts – the most biodiverse areas of the deep sea – are often trawled as they attract the greatest concentrations of commercial fish. Used as stopping off points for migratory species such as whales, as well as navigation points and nurseries, their destruction is particularly devastating for marine biodiversity.

The disturbance of the sea floor also has a disastrous impact on climate change as levels of carbon released are comparable to the carbon loss from terrestrial soils caused by farming.[113]

Why is it important?

Ocean trawling destroys marine habitats, depletes fish populations, and generates a similar volume of carbon emissions to the global aviation industry.[114] The ocean floor is the world's largest carbon store and we must leave it undisturbed if we are to halt climate change.

Scientists, ocean advocates, and some governments are calling for 30 per cent of the ocean to be protected by 2030 to save our marine resources from extractive and damaging practices. However by March 2021, only around 7 per cent of ocean area had been designated or proposed as MPAs, and only 2.7 per cent had actually been implemented.

Governments can be slow to take up the challenge because of perceived trade-offs between protection and extraction. However, studies have shown that implementing highly and fully protected areas increases the biomass of commercially important fish and invertebrates within the areas and, given time and the right conditions, can also improve productivity in fished waters outside the protected areas through expansion of the adult and larval populations from within. Strategically prioritizing which areas are protected can achieve 90 per cent of biodiversity benefits by protecting 21 per cent of the ocean, 90 per cent of food provision with just 4–5 per cent, and 90 per cent of carbon mitigation by protecting just 3.6 per cent. Prioritizing for multiple benefits can reconcile apparently conflicting priorities.

Marine scientists and advocates therefore argue that putting in place strategic conservation planning and spatial prioritization simultaneously results in benefits for biodiversity conservation and carbon storage as well as food yields.

Regenerative agriculture on land and sea is improving ocean health

A new breed of farmer is rolling out regenerative agriculture across the land with the primary target of preserving soil health. Intensive farming practices are depleting and degrading our soils at such a rate that unless we regenerate the 4 billion acres of cultivated farmland, 8 billion acres of pastureland, and 10 billion acres of forest land within 50 years, it will be impossible to feed the world, keep global warming below 2°C and halt the loss of biodiversity.[115]

There are strong interdependencies between soil health, ocean health and climate change. Exposed and depleted soils are vulnerable to our increasingly unreliable weather patterns, while heavy rain washes animal excrement, fertilizer, topsoil, and pesticides off agricultural land into the oceans, causing algal blooms and 'dead zones'.

Regenerative agriculture incorporates permaculture, organic practices, conservation tillage, cover crops, crop rotation, composting, mobile animal shelters, and pasture cropping. It puts huge amounts of carbon back into the healthy soil and plants, reduces the need for fertilizers and pesticides, and supports the restoration of biodiversity and healthy food production, with knock-on benefits for the ocean.

Regenerative farming has now reached the ocean. Regenerative ocean farming (pioneered by Greenwave[116] amongst others) involves small-scale farming of seaweed (e.g. kelp) and shellfish (e.g. clams, mussels, and oysters) using the available sunlight, plankton, and nutrients present in the water. Unlike most other forms of agriculture, there is no freshwater demand, no deforestation in the feed supply chain, no fertilizer, and very little land use.

It has been predicted that a single acre of ocean can produce 25 tons of greens and 250,000 shellfish in five months.[117] Seaweeds are high-nutrient superfoods, rich in protein, iodine, and other minerals, while oysters have a lower carbon footprint than a vegan diet.[118]

On the carbon balance side, seaweeds capture carbon, can be used as soil treatments, and when fed to cows can reduce the methane content of their burps by 58 per cent. They also have potential for algal biofuels.

Now we just need the chefs to make seaweed and shellfish palatable for a mainstream diet . . .

Chapter 7

Clothes

Fast fashion is a fast way to ocean destruction

THE ISSUE

From raw material to disposal, the lifecycle of our clothing impacts our climate and the ocean.[119] The fashion industry produces 10 per cent of all human-derived carbon emissions, is the second largest consumer of the world's water supply, and pollutes the oceans with microplastics and chemicals.[120]

....

WHAT CAN WE DO?

Fast fashion – the rapid production of high volumes of cheap clothing to meet short-term trends – manipulates our behaviour with marketing ploys that encourage us to try a new look and use shopping as an emotional crutch. Reduce temptation by unsubscribing from social media and emails that spam you with unbeatable offers on clothes you didn't even know you needed. Instead, search online for #sustainablefashion.

Take a stand against mass frenzied buying. Events like Black Friday fuel fashion waste: it's not a bargain if you don't use it.

If you like to change your style frequently, opt for upcycled, pre-loved, vintage, and charity stores, or take advantage of the share economy by renting and swapping items with friends. The environmental impact will be a fraction of newly manufactured items.

Search out responsible brands that are transparent about their environmental credentials and that are striving to be more sustainable. It may mean spending a little more on clothes, but the extra investment of time and money means we value them more and keep hold of them for longer – all of which helps our ocean.

WHY IT MATTERS

In 2010, the global clothing industry produced more than 150 billion garments, enough for more than 20 new articles of clothing for everyone on the planet[121], and the fashion industry has doubled its production in the last 15 years.[122]

Clothing fibres have been found polluting the deepest part of the ocean

THE ISSUE
Washing our clothes releases 500,000 tons of microfibres into the ocean each year, contaminating fish and sediments even in the deepest trenches and accounting for more than a third of all ocean plastic pollution.[123]

WHAT CAN WE DO?
Steer away from clothes containing synthetic fibres – key words to look out for on labels are polyester, nylon, acrylic, elastane, and neoprene. If you are unsure, you can be certain that any clothes with water resistance, stretch, or sparkle will be synthetic.

To reduce the carbon footprint of your clothes, look for recycled synthetics – recycled polyester reduces emissions by 70 per cent compared with the virgin fabric[124] – displaying the Textile Exchange logo. The new kids on the block are biosynthetics: fabrics with the performance of synthetics but made from renewable sources such as corn, beet, algae, and fungi.[125]

To reduce fibre pollution, think about how often you wash your clothes. Is it always necessary? Small marks can often be removed by sponging off, and hanging clothes up for a good airing can be enough.

Currently there are no fibre catchers in standard washing machines, so until that changes we can capture fibres in specially designed mesh bags (e.g. Guppy Friend), which also provide guidance on washing temperatures and detergents, to help us reduce our environmental impact.

WHY IT MATTERS
Fashion accounts for 20–35 per cent of microplastic flows into the ocean.[126]

Clothing dyes and chemicals are poisoning the ocean and damaging marine habitats

THE ISSUE

Around 20 per cent of global water pollution can be traced back to the textile industry.[127] The manufacturing and finishing processes in fashion production use up to 7,000 chemicals, and weak regulations in some countries allow the waste water to be dumped into the water environment.

WHAT CAN WE DO?

The fashion industry is having a massive impact on water pollution globally, and a large element of the problem is the fast fashion sector, which relies on poorly regulated supply chains that exploit the environment and workforce.We should think more critically about the companies we buy our clothes from, seeking out responsible brands. Look out for organic certifications, such as B Corp and Textile Exchange. Or look for a company that is part of the Fashion Pact, a global coalition of fashion and textile companies, including their suppliers and distributors, who have signed up to key environmental goals: stop global warming, restore biodiversity, and protect the ocean.

Toxin-free dyes are also now available, free from harmful chemicals, and create colours from non-edible agricultural or herbal waste.

If we take the time to shop responsibly we will feel good about our purchases and enjoy our clothes more, and for longer. This is just another step in our ocean hero philosophy of buying less but enjoying more.

WHY IT MATTERS

In Bangladesh, the Buriganga River is so polluted it can no longer sustain aquatic life.[128]

Producing natural fibres can be toxic, too

THE ISSUE

Deforestation occurs as 150 million trees are logged every year to produce cellulosic fabrics[129], while leather production is driving destruction of the Amazon rainforest[130,] and cotton cultivation accounts for 10 per cent of global pesticide use – around 50 per cent in developing countries.[131]

WHAT CAN WE DO?

As consumers, we have the power and responsibility to exert pressure on the fashion industry to bring about changes in textile production.

Organically produced cotton reduces pesticide and water use, but currently accounts for less than 1 per cent of global cotton production.[132] However there is growing demand from retailers and brands and we need to maintain consumer pressure to keep this trend going.

Rayon and viscose fall between natural and synthetic classification. Made from cellulose extracted from pulped wood, they still consume considerable amounts of energy and chemicals and also drive deforestation, yet 70 per cent of each tree is wasted in the pulping process.[133]

Certification schemes and campaigns can help us know where to spend our ocean-friendly pound. And thanks to Fashion Revolution, we can now ask our favourite brands #WhatsInMyClothes? on social media to help us make ocean-friendly choices.

WHY IT MATTERS

The surface area of the Aral Sea has decreased by 85 per cent due to irrigated cotton cultivation in Uzbekistan and Turkmenistan over the last 40 years.[134]

Online shopping impacts the ocean

THE ISSUE
The use of online shopping has skyrocketed in recent years, with an associated increase in vehicle traffic and packaging: up to 50 per cent of the carbon and air polluting emissions of deliveries are concentrated into the last step from depot to doorstep.[135]

WHAT CAN WE DO?
Don't despair: the impact of online shopping should be partially offset by the reduced shopping trips, and there are choices we can make to help mitigate the ocean impacts.

Choosing delivery via the postal service, which typically already comes direct to the door every day, reduces additional vehicle journeys. Collection from a convenient store that you pass regularly is also an option. And we should eliminate next- or same-day deliveries, as this results in more vehicles making more journeys using more fuel. Try to use companies that have made a commitment to low carbon transport.

Ask for goods to be sent together to reduce the packaging load, and support companies that use ocean-friendly packaging alternatives, email receipts, and return slips, and that send clothes without tags or plastic bags.

And finally, think carefully about what you buy – return packages have exactly the same carbon footprint as the outward journey.

WHY IT MATTERS
Forest conservation has been identified by the UN as 30 per cent of the climate solution. Three billion trees are cut down every year for packaging, a number projected to grow by more than 20 per cent by 2025.[136]

Less than 1 per cent of clothing fabric is recycled into new clothes[137]

THE ISSUE
On average we discard 60 per cent of our clothes within a year of buying them[138], and 40 per cent of clothes in our wardrobe are never worn.[139] This take, make, waste linear economy has led to an unnecessarily large carbon footprint and an economic loss valued at $500 billion globally.[140]

....

WHAT CAN WE DO?
We need to encourage and support the move towards a more circular fashion industry, focused on designing out waste and pollution and keeping materials and products in use.

We can reduce our own ocean impact just by keeping our clothes in circulation for longer. Research has shown that simply doubling the length of time we keep a garment could lower greenhouse gas emissions by 44 per cent.[141] And when we get bored of our clothes, we can swap them with friends or put them into the pre-loved or vintage marketplace.

Tired clothes can be upcycled with a bit of dye or by adding a few accessories. Or if your clothes have minor damage, repair them.

Look out for clothing companies that enable customers to return their garments for recycling at end of life. But don't be taken in by greenwashing, particularly from fast fashion brands: remember, at the rate of most brands' production (usually from virgin materials), it would take 12 years to recycle what they produce in 48 hours.

WHY IT MATTERS
Globally, 73 per cent of the materials used to produce clothing are landfilled or burned at the end of their life.[142]

Why is nutrient pollution a problem for the ocean and for us?

Nutrient pollution is the addition of high levels of nitrogen and phosphorus into our coastal waters via human activities, such as poorly controlled animal waste or fertilizer application in agriculture, industrial discharge, or sewage disposal.

The problem with nutrient pollution is that it enriches the water, causing excessive growth of plants and algae – a condition known as eutrophication. The negative consequences of eutrophication stem from the development of blue-green algal blooms, which stop light penetration through the water column, kill off other plant species, and prevent predatory species from hunting. They can also be toxic to people and pets, affecting recreation activities and contaminating water supplies.

The worst consequence of algal blooms in the ocean is the development of low oxygen areas, known as 'dead zones'. When the blooms die, microbial activity explodes, using up all available oxygen and creating areas devoid of oxygen (anoxic) and unable to support most marine life. The warmer the water, the less oxygen it can hold, and so climate change is exacerbating the problem, causing large-scale deoxygenation.

Why is it important?

The combined impacts of nutrient pollution and climate-change-mediated ocean warming are extending the size of known dead zones and creating new ones. 500 marine dead zones have now been recorded, up from fewer than 50 in 1950. The rapid expansion means that, added together, they now cover an area equivalent in size to the European Union.[143]

Every coastal state in the United States has recorded degradation due to nutrient pollution; this is particularly severe in the mid-Atlantic states, in the southeast, and in the Gulf of Mexico. The latter is home to one of the largest dead zones in the world, with a long-term average of around 6,000sq km, although it has reached 9,000sq km in its worst years.[144]

The dead zone in the Gulf of Oman – located between India, Iran and Oman – encompasses nearly the entire 63,700-square-mile Gulf, with conditions that are either anoxic (no oxygen) or suboxic (low oxygen).[145]

Scientists have observed that major extinction events in our planet's history have been associated with warm climates and oxygen-deficient oceans. Our current trajectory is taking us down that path but it is reversable, as has been demonstrated by dead zone recoveries in Chesapeake Bay in the US and the River Thames in the UK, when nutrient inputs from agriculture and sewage were reduced.

Ocean-friendly fashion

While the fashion industry has a significant impact on the marine environment through microplastics, nutrient and chemical pollution discharge, and carbon emissions associated with high turnover and textile production and manufacture, some companies are making significant efforts to reduce their impact. Here are just a few to whet your appetite:

Patagonia was an early leader in environmental sustainability, incorporating it into their philosophy from day one. They set their vision – 'build the best product, cause no unnecessary harm, use business to inspire and implement solutions to the environmental crisis' – and have stuck with it to this day. They continue to lead the way in sustainability, driving other competing brands like Arc'teryx and The North Face to step up to the challenge.

Rapanui is a UK clothing company on a mission to make clothing sustainable. They have developed a production process that allows them to make garments as they are ordered, in real time, meaning they only make what people need and there is no waste. New garments are made from natural materials, sourced sustainably, and using renewable energy. Every product is designed to be fully recycled – you can send end-of-life garments back to them, free of charge, and they can be fully recycled time and again into new garments – a fully circular supply chain. They are so proud of their technology-driven, zero waste, circular supply chain that they have made their platform available to anyone in the world to improve the sustainability of other businesses. It's called Teemill, and it is free.

Girlfriend Collective is one of the world's most famous sustainable activewear brands. They use fabrics made from post-consumer water bottles from landfill, and Econyl yarn obtained from fishing nets, landfill, and other ocean waste. Not only do they make their clothes from recycled materials, at end of life they take back Girlfriend pieces to turn them into brand-new pieces in a fully circular process.

Indigo Luna's range of linen, yogawear, and swimwear is made in Bali, Indonesia, in a small factory run by women. Everything from the textiles to dyes to packaging is eco-friendly. They use a Tencel fabric, derived from eucalyptus, and Econyl regenerated nylon, from fishing nets, carpets, and pre-consumer plastic waste. Their coloured dyes come from tropical plants such as indigo, mango, secang wood, and rhubarb leaves, and the process is so sustainable that even the waste is composted. Packaging is in biodegradable cassava starch bags.

Conclusion

Imagine yourself standing at the edge of the ocean. The waves lap over your feet and the undertow sucks the sand from between your toes. You pick up a stone polished smooth by the action of the surf, rolling it in your hands as your gaze moves to the horizon, blinding sun glancing off the water surface as seabirds scythe the waves. Picture the scene and feel your emotions. For some, the expanse is magical; for others, it brings fear and a sense of mystery and majesty. But for all it is deeply felt. Throughout this book we have focused on the physical ocean environment, the habitats, ecosystems, and species, the fundamental need to keep our ocean in equilibrium, to play its part in a well-functioning and balanced planet. We have said less about its value to us emotionally. Yet time spent in, on, under, and around the ocean nurtures us physically, spiritually, and creatively.

Now picture yourself again at that same spot on the edge of the ocean, at some imaginary moment in the future. But everything has changed: the surf is sluggish, thick with sediment, and iridescent with oil; islands of plastic debris break up the view to the horizon, and a jumble of lifeless birds and marine species lie tangled in marine litter along the strand line, pungent in the heat. The water level is probably surging up around your waist. The evidence is now unequivocal: human activity is warming the oceans and raising sea levels, while extreme weather events – heatwaves, droughts, floods – are becoming more and more frequent. But if we take concerted action now, we can stave off the worst consequences.

It may seem that our small individual efforts can never be enough to save our ocean from impacts as big and global as climate change and biodiversity decline. But collectively we have influence. Consumer spending represents 70 per cent of our economy, and we vote in our leaders – that is where our superpowers lie. It is time to use these to be the change we need to see, and set off a cycle of behaviour change. We can hold our politicians to account, say no to businesses that exploit our oceans, and make driving a huge gas-guzzling vehicle on urban roads unacceptable.

Of course, transformational change will require the collaboration and cooperation of governments and institutions around the world, but it is not enough to outsource the responsibility to 'them'. If we cannot be bothered to change, then why would a democratically elected government think that the big changes required are a priority? And why would businesses make the hard choices if it is not going to help them? We have to be the ones to take those first steps, the small changes that combine to become a big influence that politicians and businesses will take notice of.

Protecting and restoring the ocean is a task for more than one life and one lifetime, so we must get started now and get as many people as we know involved. It is essential for the health of the ocean and our own survival that we transition from the current position where we stand apart and exploit the ocean to one where we celebrate our interdependency, respecting and nurturing marine resources. Our ocean is worth standing up for, and this book has set out the changes we need to make. We are ready for the Grand Challenge, and it is now time to act. We need the ocean, and the ocean needs us.

References

Introduction

1. Lisa Speer, Ocean Programme Natural Resources Defence Council, CIWEM magazine, May 2020

Indoors

2. www.iucn.org/sites/dev/files/marine_plastics_ issues_brief_final_0.pdf
3. www.recyclenow.com/recycling-knowledge/ recycling-bathroom
4. See 2)
5. www.bbc.co.uk/news/uk-45732371
6. foe.scot/cutting-down-plastic-nappy/
7. See 6)
8. assets.publishing.service.gov.uk/government/ uploads/system/uploads/attachment_data/ file/291130/scho0808boir-e-e.pdf
9. www.sas.org.uk/our-work/plastic-pollution/ plastic-pollution-facts-figures/
10. wedocs.unep.org/bitstream/ handle/20.500.11822/9664/-Plastic_in_cosmetics_ Are_we_polluting_the_environment_through_our_ personal_care_-2015Plas. pdf?sequence=3&isAllowed=y
11. portals.iucn.org/library/sites/library/files/ documents/2017-002-En.pdf
12. www.theguardian.com/environment/2021/jan/28/ uk-electricity-from-renewables-outpaces-gas- and-coal-power
13. www.lse.ac.uk/granthaminstitute/explainers/why- are-household-energy-efficiency-measures- important-for-tackling-climate-change
14. www.pnas.org/content/117/32/19122
15. news.microsoft.com/innovation-stories/your- internet-habits-are-not-as-clean-as-you-think
16. www.bbc.com/future/article/20200305-why-your- internet-habits-are-not-as-clean-as-you-think
17. (See 16)
18. onlinelibrary.wiley.com/doi/abs/10.1111/jiec.12181
19. (See 16)
20. www.yumpu.com/en/document/read/31929970/pdf- causes-for-concern-chemicals-and-wildlife-wwf- uk
21. agupubs.onlinelibrary.wiley.com/doi/ full/10.1029/2018gh000146
22. www.frontiersin.org/articles/10.3389/ fmars.2020.00001/full
23. www.iucn.org/resources/issues-briefs/marine- plastics

Outdoors

24. www.nature.com/scitable/knowledge/library/ eutrophication-causes-consequences-and- controls-in-aquatic-102364466/
25. www.whoi.edu/fileserver. do?id=36113&pt=2&p=28251
26. michaelpollan.com/articles-archive/why-bother/
27. www.iucn.org/resources/issues-briefs/peatlands- and-climate-change
28. www.theguardian.com/environment/2019/feb/10/ plummeting-insect-numbers-threaten-collapse- of-nature
29. www.sciencedirect.com/science/article/pii/ S0006320718313636

30. besjournals.onlinelibrary.wiley.com/doi/10.1111/1365-2745.13598

31. (See 28)

32. (See 29)

33. www.nature.com/articles/s41598-020-69461-6

34. www.unep.org/news-and-stories/story/global-light-pollution-affecting-ecosystems-what-can-we-do

35. www.nhm.ac.uk/discover/light-pollution

36. https://www.mcsuk.org/news/great-british-beach-clean-results-2019/

37. pubs.acs.org/doi/full/10.1021/acs.est.8b06984

38. birdlife.org.au/documents/Dogs_and_Beach-nesting_Birds_Management_Solutions_Nov2018.pdf

39. www.gov.uk/government/publications/faecal-contamination-challenges-for-the-water-environment

40. mcc.jrc.ec.europa.eu/documents/201709180716.pdf

41. www.lessplastic.org.uk/10-marine-litter-facts-how-reduce-plastic-pollution/

42. (See 40)

43. ioc.unesco.org/news/new-global-ocean-science-report-voices-concern-over-inadequacy-funding-ocean-research

44. oceanconservancy.org/wp-content/uploads/2019/09/Final-2019-ICC-Report.pdf

45. www.sciencedirect.com/science/article/pii/S0048969718306442?via%3Dihub

46. www.ipcc.ch/srocc/chapter/summary-for-policymakers/

47. www.iucn.org/resources/issues-briefs/ocean-warming

48. www.imperial.ac.uk/media/imperial-co.llege/grantham-institute/public/publications/briefing-papers/Ocean-heat-uptake---Grantham-BP-15.pdf

49. (See 47)

Transport

50. www.bbc.com/future/article/20200317-climate-change-cut-carbon-emissions-from-your-commute

51. innovativemobility.org/wp-content/uploads/2016/07/Impactsofcar2go_FiveCities_2016.pdf

52. www.who.int/health-topics/air-pollution#tab=tab_1

53. (See 50)

54. www.qld.gov.au/transport/public/bicycle-riding/benefits-of-riding

55. www.transportenvironment.org/challenges/air-quality/

56. www.bbc.co.uk/news/science-environment-49759626

57. www.carbonbrief.org/factcheck-how-electric-vehicles-help-to-tackle-climate-change

58. www.driving.co.uk/car-clinic/should-i-buy-an-electric-car-now/

59. (See 56)

60. (See 11)

61. www.ncbi.nlm.nih.gov/pmc/articles/PMC5664766/

62. (See 11)

63. www.greenchoices.org/green-living/transport/air-travel
64. www.bbc.co.uk/news/science-environment-49349566
65. (See 63)

On Holiday

66. www.wwf.org.uk/updates/tourists-cause-almost-40-spike-plastic-entering-mediterranean-sea-each-summer
67. www.outdoorswimmingsociety.com/ocean-friendly-river-friendly-sunscreens/
68. oceanservice.noaa.gov/news/sunscreen-corals.html
69. (See 68)
70. archive.mccip.org.uk/media/1896/2013arc_sciencereview_29_tmarr_final.pdf
71. www.researchgate.net/publication/271449937_Tourism_impact_on_coastal_environment
72. www.researchgate.net/publication/328676001_The_radical_outcomes_of_tourism_development_on_the_natural_environment_in_coastal_areas
73. (See 70)
74. www.bbc.co.uk/news/magazine-14107381#:~:text=Whale%20watching%20can%20have%20an,whales%2C%20putting%20everyone%20at%20risk.
75. worldcetaceanalliance.org/wp-content/uploads/2019/07/WCA-Global-Best-Practice-Guidance-Whale-Watch.pdf
76. (See 75)
77. defenders.org/sites/default/files/publications/ecological-impacts-and-practices-of-the-coral-reef-wildlife-trade.pdf
78. www.science.org/doi/full/10.1126/science.aba4658

At Work

79. www.ellenmacarthurfoundation.org/case-studies
80. www.centerforecotechnology.org/is-working-from-home-better-for-the-environment/
81. www.ft.com/greenpensions
82. (See 81)
83. www.fishforward.eu/en/project/by-catch/

Food

84. www.edie.net/news/5/WRAP--Two-thirds-of-Brits-don-t-see-link-between-food-waste-and-climate-change/
85. (See 84)
86. www.sciencedirect.com/science/article/abs/pii/S0921344914002626#!
87. www.sciencedirect.com/science/article/abs/pii/S092134490800133X
88. www.bbc.com/future/article/20200224-how-cutting-your-food-waste-can-help-the-climate
89. www.greenpeace.org/static/planet4-international-stateless/2019/11/018c3eae-30x30-ocean-climate-report-greenpeace-2019.pdf
90. www.reuters.com/article/us-mangroves-idUSBRE8AD1EG20121114
91. www.bbc.co.uk/news/science-environment-57436143
92. www.nature.com/articles/s41893-021-00720-8

93. www.msc.org/what-we-are-doing/our-approach/what-is-sustainable-fishing?gclid=EAlaIQobChMInPn15Jrp7gIV4oBQBh0EXQZFEAAYASAAEgJX9_D_BwE

94. (See 90)

95. www.bbcgoodfood.com/howto/guide/facts-about-food-miles

96. (See 95)

97. www.theguardian.com/environment/2021/jun/10/takeaway-food-and-drink-litter-dominates-ocean-plastic-study-shows

98. www.nature.com/articles/s41893-021-00720-8

99. www.geochemicalperspectivesletters.org/article1829/

100. (See 9)

101. core.ac.uk/download/pdf/77082802.pdf

102. www.sciencedirect.com/science/article/pii/S0959378014000338

103. (See 101)

104. onlybuyvegan.com/wp-content/uploads/2017/07/Spotlight_-Livestock-impacts-on-the-environment.pdf

105. ourworldindata.org/environmental-impacts-of-food

106. pubmed.ncbi.nlm.nih.gov/19587236/

107. www.ipcc.ch/srocc/chapter/chapter-5/

108. www.who.int/news-room/fact-sheets/detail/pesticide-residues-in-food

109. (See 89)

110. (See 106)

111. assets.publishing.service.gov.uk/government/uploads/system/uploads/attachment_data/file/957629/Dasgupta_Review_-_Headline_Messages.pdf

112. doi.org/10.1038/s41586-021-03371-z

113. (See 112)

114. (See 112)

115. regenerationinternational.org/why-regenerative-agriculture/

116. www.greenwave.org/

117. www.yesmagazine.org/environment/2016/04/04/the-seas-will-save-us-how-an-army-of-ocean-farmers-is-starting-an-economic-revolution

118. esajournals.onlinelibrary.wiley.com/doi/full/10.1002/fee.1822

Clothes

119. www.fashionrevolution.org/nature-in-freefall/

120. www.businessinsider.com/fast-fashion-environmental-impact-pollution-emissions-waste-water-2019-10?r=US&IR=T

121. matteroftrust.org/wp-content/uploads/2015/10/SustainableApparelMaterials.pdf

122. wtvox.com/fashion/fashion-waste/

123. (See 120)

124. textileexchange.org/2025-recycled-polyester-challenge/

125. aboutbiosynthetics.org/

126. www.mckinsey.com/industries/retail/our-insights/state-of-fashion

127. (See 126)

128. www.greenamerica.org/unraveling-fashion-industry/unpacking-toxic-textiles

129. canopyplanet.org/wp-content/uploads/2019/02/CanopyStyle-5th-Anniversary-Report.pdf

130. journals.sagepub.com/doi/
    full/10.1177/194008291300600309

131. d2ouvy59p0dg6k.cloudfront.net/downloads/
    cotton_for_printing_long_report.pdf

132. (See 131)

133. (See 130)

134. (See 131)

135. Wardley, T., The Eco Hero Handbook (The Ivy
    Press, 2021), p.132

136. canopyplanet.org/campaigns/pack4good/

137. (See 120)

138. (See 122)

139. unece.org/fileadmin/DAM/RCM_Website/
    RFSD_2018_Side_event_sustainable_fashion.pdf

140. www.mckinsey.com/~/media/mckinsey/
    industries/retail/our%20insights/the%20
    state%20of%20fashion%202020%20
    navigating%20uncertainty/the-state-of-fashion-
    2020-final.pdf

141. www.europarl.europa.eu/RegData/etudes/
    BRIE/2019/633143/EPRS_BRI(2019)633143_
    EN.pdf

142. https://ellenmacarthurfoundation.org/topics/
    fashion/overview

143. www.researchgate.net/publication/322292328_
    Declining_oxygen_in_the_global_ocean_and_
    coastal_waters

144. www.noaa.gov/media-release/large-dead-zone-
    measured-in-gulf-of-mexico

145. e360.yale.edu/digest/scientists-confirm-florida
    sized-dead-zone-in-the-gulf-of-oman

Index

A

acidification, ocean 51, 80, 92
agriculture 106–9, 112, 114–15, 130, 131
air quality and pollution 58–9, 61, 127
air travel 64–5, 103, 113
algal blooms 35, 107, 114, 130
anthrophony 80
antibacterial products 25
Attenborough, David 11, 67

B

B Corp businesses 31, 123
baby-care products 16–17
baby wipes 17, 47
bags 19, 29, 49, 63, 73, 105
bathroom plastics 14, 15
batteries 60–1
beaches 44–5, 49
beauty products 14, 15
biodiversity 49
   deep sea 61, 66, 67
   importance of oceans for 6, 10, 92–3
   loss of 11, 35, 61, 92–3, 112
   ocean warming 10, 51
   restoring 41, 113, 114
   seagrass 94
biophony 80

birds 45, 46, 47
body boards 73
businesses 31, 94, 123
bycatch 95, 112

C

carbon: blue carbon 67
   carbon footprints 15, 17, 23, 29, 37, 57, 88, 89, 102–3, 121
   emissions 21, 23, 61, 89, 103, 113, 119, 127, 132
   ocean trawling and 112, 113
   storage of 10, 27, 109
cars 23, 56–63, 65, 88–9
   maintenance 26–7
   tyres 19, 29, 61, 62–3
chemicals 24–5, 29, 37, 108–9, 119, 122, 123
   fertilizers 34–5, 107, 114, 130
   pesticides 109
circular economy 87, 129
cleaning products 24–5
clothes 19, 29, 31, 63, 116–33
community action 52–3
commutes 88–9
compost 35, 39, 99
computer equipment 86–7
conservation 48–9, 82–3, 113
consumerism 110–11

coral 43, 51, 75, 79, 92, 94, 95, 109, 112
cotton 125
currents 68, 69
cycling 57, 59, 89

D

dairy 106–7
data storage, online 22–3
dead zones 34–5, 107, 114, 130–1
deep sea minerals 66–7
deforestation 125
DIY 26–7
dogs 44–5
dolphins 24, 25, 79, 81, 95
dyes 122, 123

E

ecosystems 83
   coastal 51, 52–3, 77, 79
   coral reefs 51, 75, 79
   deep sea 66
   disruption of 29, 43, 93
   insects and 40–1
   marine protected areas 7
   overfishing 100, 101
   seagrass 94
ecotourism 82–3
electric vehicles (EVs) 60–1

electricity 21, 68–9
emails 23
energy: consumption 20–1, 23, 36–7, 89
   renewable 68–9
Environment Agency 17, 45
eutrophication 130

F
faecal contamination 45
fashion 19, 29, 31, 63, 116–33
   fast fashion 118–19, 123
fertilizers 34–5, 107, 114, 130
Fiji 53
Finisterre 31
fish and fishing 7, 53, 83
   bycatch 95, 112
   ocean trawling 112–13
   overfishing 6, 10, 30, 52, 80, 92, 100–1
food 36–7, 96–115
fossil fuels 50, 68, 91
fruit 37

G
gaming 23
geophony 80
Girlfriend Collective 133
Great Pacific Garbage Patch 28
greenhouse gases 50, 59, 64–5, 89, 99, 107, 129
greenwashing 82, 91, 129

H
Hawaii 53
heating 21, 89
holidays 70–83
home working 88–9

I
Indigo Luna 133
insects 40–1
insulation 21, 89
internet 22–3

K
Kay, Tom 30, 31
kelp beds 10, 26, 115

L
LEDs (light emitting diodes) 21, 43
lighting 21, 43, 103
litter 47, 73, 105
livestock 107

M
MacArthur, Dame Ellen 30
mangroves 10, 51, 101, 109
manure 39

marine life 29, 42–3, 51, 59, 63, 78, 81, 82, 94, 112
marine protected areas (MPAs) 7, 52
marine research 48–9
Mars Assisted Reef Restoration System (MARRS) 95
meat 106–7
methane 66, 107, 115
microbeads 19
microplastics 18–19, 29, 61, 62–3, 73, 119, 120, 121, 132
motor oil 27

N
nappies 17
natural fibres 124–5
noise pollution 103
nutrient pollution 130–1, 132

O
ocean mining 60–1, 66–7, 92
Ocean Thermal Energy Conversion (OTEC) 69
oceans: importance of 9–10
   sea levels 20, 21, 51
   warming of 10, 50–1, 92
office equipment 86–7
online data storage 22–3
online shopping 126–7

organic food 109
osmotic power 69
oxygen 9, 27, 29
  deoxygenation 51, 64–5, 107, 130, 131

P
packaging 31, 47, 73, 104–5, 127
Patagonia 132
peatland 38–9
pensions 90–1
personal care products 14, 19, 73
pesticides 109
petroleum 28, 29
phthalates 25
plastic 14–15, 19, 28–31
  bags 19, 29, 49, 63, 73, 105
  microplastics 18–19, 29, 61, 62–3, 73, 119, 120, 132
  packaging 31, 47, 73, 104–5
  pollution 14–15, 28–9, 94, 105
  waste 72–3
  wildlife and 46–7
pollinators 37, 41
pollution 52, 77, 107
  air 58–9, 127
  cars 57
  light 103
  litter 47
  marine life and 42–3

microplastics 18–19, 29, 61, 62–3, 73, 119, 120, 132
noise 80, 81, 103
nutrient 34–5, 37, 130–1, 132
plastic 14–15, 28–9, 94, 105
Puerto Morelos reef 52
Pugh, Lewis 6–8, 30–1

R
Rapanui 132
rare earth metals 60–1, 66
recycling clothes 128–9
reefs 43, 51, 52, 75, 82, 92, 94, 95, 109
regenerative agriculture 114–15

S
sanitary products 15
science 48–9
sea levels, rising 20, 21, 51
seagrass 26, 27, 51, 53, 94, 109
seaweeds 115
sharks 83
shopping, online 126–7
Sky Ocean Rescue 94
social media 76, 77, 111, 119
solar power 89
soundscapes, ocean 80–1
souvenirs 79
sunscreen 74–5

sustainable clothing 132
synthetic polymers 19

T
technology 21, 23
texts 23
tidal energy 68–9
toothpaste 15
tourism 72–3, 76–9
transport 23, 54–69, 88–9, 103, 127
trees 127
Triodos 95
tyres 19, 29, 61, 62–3

V
vegetables 37

W
washing clothes 121
waste 72–3, 86–7, 129
wave power 68–9
whales 81, 83, 95, 112
white goods 21
wildlife 43, 45, 46–7, 37
wind power 68, 69
wipes 17, 47
work 84–95

Acknowledgments

This book could not have been written without the help, support, inspiration and love given to me by my family and the many friends, colleagues, and activists in the movement to protect the ocean that is integral to our survival.

Firstly, I would like to thank my commissioning editor, Chloe, my copyeditor Rachel, and illustrator Melanie, as well as the rest of the team at Ivy Press. You made this book happen.

Secondly, I would like to give a special shout-out to the friends who sustained me with ocean adventures, keeping me inspired and sane throughout the writing of the book. They are: my amazing channel swimming team, the Salty Selkies, Linda, Fiona, Sean, Elise, Stella, and Claire who have provided companionship, support, entertainment and drive through many cold and hard hours in English waters, salty and fresh. We all owe gratitude to Christine our fantastic coach, muse, and motivator who brought us all together, and calmly gives us confidence to achieve more than we believe we can. There are many other channel swimmers who have been there through the journey: Oceanides team, Emma, Ness, Hildy and Rebecca, Amanda, and the Girls Alive teams, and Heather from Portsmouth Uni with her wonderful helpers.

I'm very grateful to Lewis Pugh who is inspiring so many people with his crazy swimming exploits which raise a much-needed awareness on the importance and plight of our ocean. Your influence is great and you are making a difference all around the ocean and the world. Thank you.

There are the countless people I have had the pleasure of working with and learning with on ocean matters over the years who have been an ongoing inspiration in my thirst for knowledge on the marine environment. I would like to thank those I have been talking to about the book as it grew, who shared ideas and thoughts and new directions to take, including current and former colleagues, friends and family, activists, and passers-by.

Finally, and most importantly, I want to thank my family. My parents, who introduced me to 'our' stretch of the salty world and started that love affair, giving me the best childhood anyone could dream of. My brothers and sister, who shared those beginnings and continue to support and inspire me. My husband who is just gorgeous and an unfailingly positive force in all I do. My 4 girls, who are wonderful and each bring their own special light to the world. Between them, all their cousins, and their friends, they give me hope and confidence that the next generation are a safe pair of hands to take on the challenges of our global future. I dedicate this book to them all.